Dear Jan:

Riding

with the

Wind

Best Wishes.

Jan

D1435779

Our Journey Through China, 1931–1949

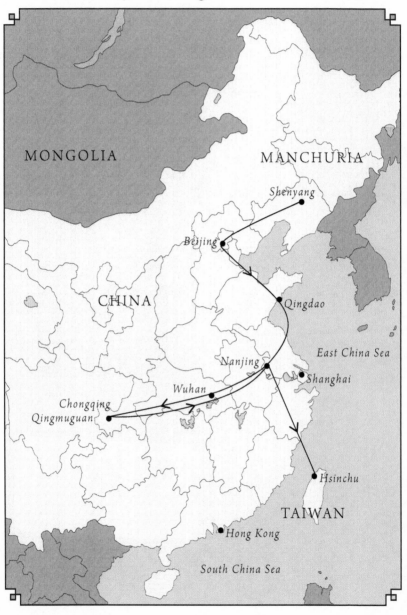

Riding

with the

Wind

THREE GENERATIONS OF MY FAMILY IN CHINA

Fay Hoh Yin

EDITED BY MONONA YIN

Yin Imprints
yinimprints@gmail.com

Cover painting and calligraphy by the author's mother, Tze Kao
Cover design by Sally Rinehart, sallyrinehart.com
Interior design by Sally Rinehart and
Colleen Shaheen, wdrbookdesign.com
Author photographs by Thomas Fichter

Visit the author's webpage at fayhohyin.com
for discussion guide and other resources.

Printed in the United States of America
First Printing, April 2017

ISBN: 978-0-998-9064-0-9
eISBN: 978-0-998-9064-1-6

In loving memory of my parents,
that they might live on
in the hearts of my children
and grandchildren

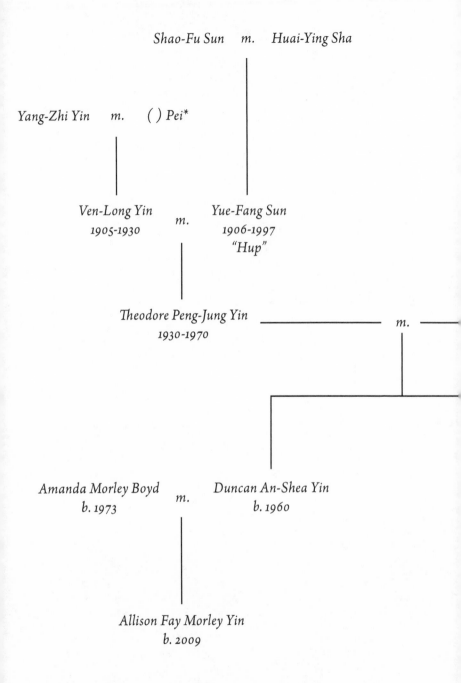

Shao-Fu Sun   *m.*   Huai-Ying Sha

Yang-Zhi Yin   *m.*   ( ) Pei*

Ven-Long Yin   *m.*   Yue-Fang Sun
1905-1930   1906-1997
                              "Hup"

Theodore Peng-Jung Yin ————————— *m.* ——
1930-1970

Amanda Morley Boyd   *m.*   Duncan An-Shea Yin
b. 1973   b. 1960

Allison Fay Morley Yin
b. 2009

* Given name unknown, as was common for Chinese women

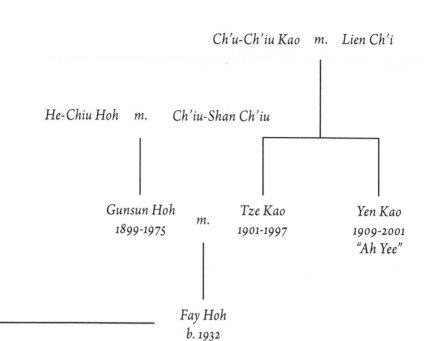

Ch'u-Ch'iu Kao   m.   Lien Ch'i

He-Chiu Hoh   m.   Ch'iu-Shan Ch'iu

Gunsun Hoh
1899-1975   m.   Tze Kao
1901-1997   Yen Kao
1909-2001
"Ah Yee"

Fay Hoh
b. 1932

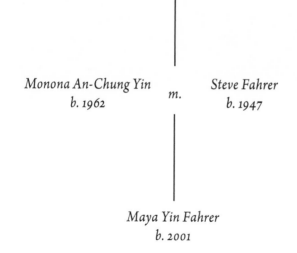

Monona An-Chung Yin
b. 1962   m.   Steve Fahrer
b. 1947

Maya Yin Fahrer
b. 2001

Author's Note

I grew up with the Wade-Giles system of Romanization but recognize that Pinyin is the worldwide standard today and more intuitive for non-Chinese speakers. Therefore, I have used Pinyin for all place names except Hsinchu (Xinzhu) in Taiwan, as that is its official name.

For the names of family members, I have generally retained the Wade-Giles spelling that they used themselves; other names are rendered in Pinyin. Please note that Chinese names begin with the family name but I have reversed the order according to the Western custom. My family's names are cross-referenced in Chinese, Pinyin and Wade-Giles on page 214.

Finally, I have included many translated Chinese sayings in this book. For those who are interested, the original versions are shown on page 217.

Contents

Preface

by Monona A. Yin

On December 12, 2015, my mother said tearful goodbyes to us from her bed at Memorial Sloan Kettering Hospital. She had been diagnosed with angioimmunoblastic T-cell lymphoma sixteen months earlier: a rare and intractable form of cancer. Mom had dutifully completed six months of chemotherapy in Delaware, and it appeared to have done its job. We were cautiously optimistic that she could resume living alone in her serene condo, enjoying her orchids, writing, investing, spending occasional time with friends, and, most of all, dancing at least twice a week. For almost a year, our wish came true (except for the dancing), but then Mom became alarmingly weak in October.

We decided to seek a second opinion at a world-class cancer center but was it too late? My brother Duncan drove Mom, now tethered to an oxygen tank, to New York for testing. I had to use a wheelchair to get her upstairs. She had never been so frail. After the tests, Mom's blood pressure dropped to 96/46 so she was admitted to the hospital. That evening so much fluid had accumulated in her lungs that she could barely breathe. Between gasps, she told me that she was done struggling. After eighty-three years of surviving war, leaving China, making her way in a new country, losing my father at age thirty-seven, raising two kids, caring for both my dying grandmothers and always being our rock, it appeared that Mom's time had run out.

It was a heartrending scene. When my fourteen-year-old daughter Maya arrived, Mom couldn't hold back her sobs. "I'm so sorry I won't see you grow up. I'm sorry I won't see you graduate or get married." Maya had always been my mother's pride and joy, her hope for the future. Now the poor girl was devastated by these sudden declarations from her beloved Nai Nai.

Although we had all been coming to terms with Mom's mortality for months, the shock and pain were still overwhelming. For me, it was made worse by the fact that she and I, who had always been close, had gained a new level of trust during her illness. We had hashed out her end-of-life wishes amid many tears, and I had promised to make sure they were honored. Losing her now would blast an even bigger hole in my heart than before, when our lives were more separate.

I grabbed the young doctor on duty, one I'd never seen before, and asked him to "stop everything." He assented but then ordered another blood test, so I had to put my foot down. My mind flashed back to the books on death and dying that I'd read and discussed with Mom. Yes, it was true. Hospital staff always default to more treatment. You've got to fight hard to make them stop. I girded myself for a wretched night of wanting to save my mother yet being sworn to do the opposite.

Then something miraculous happened: a nurse from Hospice of New York returned my call and, hearing my distress, kindly offered to come to the hospital. By that time, I had learned to accept any proffered help without shame. She arrived and swiftly advised us of our options, but then said, "Let me go talk to your mother." After fifteen minutes, during which we agonized over Mom's DNR ("do not resuscitate" order), Nurse Tracy emerged and declared that, based on her experience, Mom was not going to die that night, nor anytime soon.

What?! It took a few minutes to absorb her words but then, "Goodbye surrender, hello fighting spirit!" I grabbed whoever was on duty and reversed my previous order. Over the next four weeks, the MSK lymphoma, cardiology and pulmonary teams worked together to bring Mom back from the brink. They administered steroids, transfused many units of blood, stabilized her platelet count, drained her lungs, optimized her diuretic, treated her infections, and gave her "every test MSK has."

I still can't believe how hard the doctors and nurses fought to save an eighty-three-year-old. I'll be forever grateful to them. Mom transferred to a rehabilitation center on January 15, where she stayed another month building up her strength. On February 12, she finally moved into my home in Brooklyn and—knock wood—has only been back to MSK for check-ups. On those occasions we always eat in the cafeteria—the best value meal in town and a comforting second home to us.

I prize the awareness that comes from being well acquainted with death. Like Emily in *Our Town*, I now realize how immeasurably precious just being alive is. In this past year, I have learned what a difference my mom's daily presence makes. Before, Steve, Maya and I would often eat our meals around the L of the kitchen counter but, with Mom in the mix, the four of us eat at the dining table. It's a whole different experience with a tablecloth, big dishes to pass around, and time to linger and talk. There is often a moment when I look across at my mother and daughter, eating the food I have cooked and laughing about some little thing, when I am flooded with gratitude. I know that when Maya is grown and on her own, she will remember her grandmother as an intimate, someone with whom she shared many joyful times, and that gives me solace for whatever is to come.

In Chapter Two of this memoir, my great-grandmother Kao mourns the rupture when my grandmother moves to Shanghai for college. She rightly believes that her daughter will never live as her foremothers did, raising children and managing a *da jiating* (multi-generational household). Yet Great-Grandmother might have been comforted to know that her daughter carried on a Chinese tradition that stretches back centuries. Whenever a dynasty became corrupt or weak and "lost the mandate of heaven," younger patriots always sought to restore the country. Inspired by the same goal, my grandparents became educators who worked to throw off foreign domination by invigorating Chinese youth. They studied in the West but returned home, devoting their lives to modernizing China.

Moving in the other direction, I was fortunate to reconnect with this lineage. I was born and grew up in Delaware but took a break from college to study Chinese in Taiwan. I spent fourteen months at my still vigorous grandmother's side, imbibing her idealism and fierce ethnic pride. When my mother came to bring me home, she teasingly dubbed me "Little Taiwan" because I had indeed become a native, taking her to eat street food that my grandmother deemed unsafe.

When I returned to the States, I experienced culture shock. For months, everything seemed impossibly clean and orderly and enormous compared to the smelly chaos of Taiwan. I missed the food, the language, and being one limb of a large family tree with deep roots. Back at school, I studied labor, ethnic, and women's history and literature. I graduated in 1985 and moved to New York City to "serve the people." Thirty years later, I'm still working on behalf of immigrants and refugees, but my life would have been very different had I not struggled to integrate my Chinese and American selves.

When I became a mother myself in 2001, I wondered how I would connect Maya to our family in China, past and present. It has not been easy given the distance but I've made peace with the fact that she will have to weave her own ties as I did. Thankfully, this memoir makes the job easier, filled as it is with priceless stories that even "Little Taiwan" didn't learn. What's more remarkable is that Mom's stories will remain undimmed for Maya's children and their children.

It's a tragedy that my father never lived to see Duncan and me grow up to have our own families. He was a man with a huge appetite for life who would have given us the world instead of a dark cloud. I'm relieved that this book restores his place in our annals, reclaims his promise and accomplishments. He was smart, ambitious, and worked ferociously to realize his dreams, like so many immigrants. I feel tender toward the young Ted in these pages, who shared a special bond with his widowed mother and clawed his way to America. I am astonished that I'm now old enough to be that man's mother.

For many years, none of us could speak about Daddy without crying. Even what we called him seemed frozen in time. He never aged in our grainy memories, always the dashing young man smiling at his future. Watching *Mad Men* reminded me so much of Daddy with his well-cut suits and skinny ties. He was a star chemist at DuPont, married to my gorgeous and capable mom, and Tiger Dad to two bright kids. In 1963, he finally brought his mother over from Hong Kong, and the five of us seemed to have a limitless future.

It was the height of the post-war boom, and everyone we knew was on the up escalator. My parents were uncommonly blessed with two incomes and a live-in babysitter. We lived in a white suburb with great public schools, unlocked doors, and only a dim awareness of the Civil Rights Movement and Vietnam War.

My brother and I considered ourselves regular American kids, even though we got called "Ching Chong Chinaman" on a regular basis. In first grade, an older special-ed class adopted me as its punching bag, and it took months to make them stop. After school, we played kickball, football or baseball with the other kids in the neighborhood, and watched *Gilligan's Island*.

DuPont was churning out Nylon, Teflon and other miracle products. My dad got a patent for a sound deadening polymer that had its own TV commercial: in slow motion, you see Hercules swing a mallet toward a huge gong. Long seconds pass while you hold your breath. At the dramatic moment of contact, all you hear is a puny "thunk." Brilliant job by some Don Draper. Mom told us later that Dad's compound was used in submarines and dishwashers. In 1966, she also got a job at the DuPont Experimental Station, a small city with fifty buildings and thousands of workers. On weekends, though, the place was deserted; both Duncan and I learned to drive there.

After my grandmother, Hup, arrived in 1963, my parents started traveling for two weeks every summer. They were making up for their penniless student days. My mom told me years later that she "lived for those two weeks," which I can now understand only too well. In 1969, Daddy was being groomed to be a manager, and my parents bought land on which to build a new house. First, though, he arranged to take a sabbatical in Taiwan for six months so we could spend time with my mom's family. I was seven and Duncan was nine.

My parents enrolled us in Taipei American School with the children of GIs and expat business people. I resented the fact that the military kids could buy Frosted Flakes at the PX, but I couldn't.

When Valentine's Day rolled around, it took me hours to cut and glue my own cards while they had some kind of secret channel to North America. I was dumbfounded the next day when I got a fistful of those store-bought valentines that come twenty-five to a pack.

My teacher Mrs. Ulmer was kind, and the kids were friendly enough. They sent me a thick pack of chatty letters after we returned to the U.S. In hindsight, I realize they only did that because I was the kid whose dad had died. I must say that our time in Taiwan in '69 didn't make me feel a whole lot more Chinese. I was still a minority in my classes, and we spoke English at home and school.

Our lives were supposed to continue on this frictionless path upward. But one night near the end of our stay, while we kids slept, our charmed life came to an end in the family bathroom. A leaking tank of gas killed my unsuspecting father while he bathed, obliterating a lifetime of striving in a few silent minutes. We lost our immunity and our innocence with no chance for a do-over. What if Mom had checked on Daddy a few minutes earlier? What if Daddy had turned off the gas before getting in the tub? What if Taiwan had had decent plumbing and emergency services? What if? What if? These tortured questions reverberated for many years, but the outcome never changed.

I give my mother and Hup enormous credit for having the courage to return to the U.S. It would have been easy to stay in Taiwan and let my mom's formidable parents take charge. But the two women who became my primary parents opted for a life on their own terms in a country that didn't shun widows. They stayed together another twenty-seven years, creating an unconventional marriage that gave Duncan and me a secure and loving home. I don't know many people who could have pulled that off with such grace, cooperation and mutual respect. But they did, and my brother and I can never repay that debt.

Bringing this book into being has been the silver lining of all those fear-filled days and nights at Mom's bedside. But for her medical team and good health insurance, neither she nor her memoirs would be here today.

Sitting doggedly at her laptop day after day, Mom has shown herself to be a real writer, determined "to find the right word, to choose, finally, the one that is the most exact, most incisive," in the words of Jhumpa Lahiri, one of her favorite authors. I find it extraordinary that Mom paints her Chinese childhood so vividly in lyrical English prose. Like any true author, Mom is willing to write and rewrite until she feels the rush of satisfaction from getting the nuances right.

My mother's mother was a noted public speaker. She commanded the attention of many thousands of students over a seventy-year teaching career. My mother chose a different path, doing research in a lab and waiting until her fifties to begin writing these deeply personal essays. I thought I knew her through and through, yet this past year has been a revelation. I've seen her blossom as an artist and as a person.

Life is unpredictable. And sad. And unbearably beautiful. After going to hell and back, Mom and I have both shed a lot of our demons. You've got to travel light when you can only carry the important things. I thank the universe that I survived many rocky years to have this sweet one with my mother. She gave me life and she still gives me life, every day.

March 2017
Brooklyn, New York

Introduction

My Dear Children,

After I retired in 1991, the urge to tell you about my family and my childhood in China bubbled up and became irresistible. Over the next twenty-plus years, I worked on these stories on and off whenever the mood struck me. In 1995, I began taking writing classes at the Academy of Lifelong Learning, University of Delaware. There my teachers and fellow students encouraged me to continue telling stories about "my China."

I think of these pieces as our family's legacy and my gifts to you. Other than describing my own experiences, these are the stories my parents, my aunt, and my mother-in-law told me. Both my parents had illustrious careers and many articles were written about them. My father also wrote his autobiography. These became references for my writing. I couldn't help but include my parents' public lives but, more importantly, I wanted you to see them as loving parents and your grandparents. I could only include a few stories from Daddy's side of the family because, even though I lived with his mother for thirty-five years, I know much less of the Yin and Sun family histories.

I want to share with you the relatives you barely knew or never met—their lives, struggles, sacrifices, and survival in a tumultuous, changing time in China. I also want you to learn more about your young father, whose life was cut short in an accident when you were little. It only became obvious to me after I finished writing that each generation passed on their love to the next in the best way they knew how. This love fortified their children in their own times of hardship and became the strength behind their survival.

I want you to know the China I remember. As I was writing, I realized that "my China" had ceased to be around the early 1950s when I left; it bears no resemblance to the China that has progressed and changed relentlessly for the last sixty years. It cannot be found in today's Taiwan either, where I lived for two years. Still, I am partial to my China as a time when life was slower paced, family was at the center of everything, and honoring one's elders and keeping one's promises were revered practices. Three-quarters of the nineteen years that I lived in China took place during the war with Japan. We were refugees in our own country—constantly running, dodging, and trying to stay ahead of the invading Japanese army. We were lucky that nobody in our family was killed. In spite of that, I had a wonderful childhood and many sweet memories. Against a backdrop of chaos and terror, my parents somehow managed to make happy times.

This, then, is my China with all its blemishes and beauty. I hope you pass these stories onto your own children and grandchildren.

Riding

with the

Wind

ONE

Grandfather Hoh and His Sons

Traditional Chinese house © Rafael Ben-Ari/Alamy

My paternal grandfather Hoh was the ninth son of his father who lovingly nicknamed him "my favorite ninth dragon." Grandfather Hoh was the only one of my four grandparents whom I knew at all. He and Step-Grandmother came to live with my parents and me in Chongqing in southwest China in 1940, during the Sino-Japanese War. In 1945, after the war ended, they returned to their ancestral home in Caodian, Jiangsu Province, on China's east coast.

Grandfather Hoh was in his seventies when I was eight. A small and compact man, he always dressed neatly, with every hair in place. Against his graying hair, his eyebrows remained dark and heavy, sentinels to his piercing eyes. He was extremely active and agile for his age. In the winter, he wore padded cotton pants that were bound at the ankles. He would point to them and say, "You see, they keep me warm and unencumbered, a far cry from Western clothing."

Grandfather's special gift was beautiful calligraphy, each character no bigger than the size of a rice kernel. People marveled at the good eyesight and steady hands that allowed him to write so well at his age. They often asked for his work to frame and display in their homes. Proud of his calligraphy, he included his signature and age on each scroll.

Grandfather's writing desk, on which calligraphy brushes lined up in their containers like so many little soldiers, dominated his room. He not only collected seals but was accomplished in the art of seal carving as well. Of his large collection, the best seals stood next to the red ink pad, and Grandfather had a story to tell about each one. My interest usually focused on the shelf where a green jar decorated with a bamboo painting held preserved plums, a red one with apple blossoms contained salted peanuts, and one or two other jars offered the surprises of the day.

Grandfather taught me Chinese poetry and, although I understood little of its meaning, I worked hard to memorize the verses because the rewards were immediate and delicious. Even if I failed to remember a line or two, Grandfather would help me out. He always recited with great style. His voice rose and fell with the rhyme, melodious like a song, one moment *andante*, and the next *allegretto*, while his upper body swayed left and right with eyes closed, enraptured with the beauty of the poems. Years later when Grandfather was near death, he often made mumbling sounds. Second Uncle attended him and, thinking that his father had some important message to pass on, bent and struggled to hear him—only to realize that his father was reciting his favorite poems.

Relatives often told me I was lucky to know Grandfather when he had mellowed in his old age, for he was famed for his fiery temper in his younger days. One of the often-told stories described Grandfather jumping up from his siesta bed, chasing after the rooster that had repeatedly interrupted his afternoon nap, and actually catching it and breaking its neck. I also remember hearing Grandfather yell at my father. Even in his twilight years, he angered quickly. But fortunately, his thunder and lightning disappeared quickly too, and a few hours later his smile would shine anew.

On lazy summer evenings, Father loved to fill in some of the family history for me. For generations the Hoh family had owned land in Caodian, Jiangsu Province. My great-grandfather reportedly owned nine hundred Chinese *mu* of land (equivalent to five hundred forty acres). My grandfather, with each of his eight brothers, inherited about one hundred *mu*, which afforded them a comfortable living. The land was worked by small farmers who paid the Hohs a yearly rent. If the farmers fared well, then they would make a special trip to the Hoh family house at the end of the year bearing extra gifts: pigs and chickens, huge bucketfuls of dried vegetables, and a few delicious pheasants.

The Hoh males, along with some relatives and neighbors, all went to "family school" to study Chinese classics. A hired teacher, usually a studious but poor relative, ran the one-room school. The simple curriculum consisted of mostly classics, including history, philosophy, ethics, and calligraphy. Poetry was considered a plaything and was tolerated as a form of recreation. The age of the students ranged from six to eighteen, but little attention was paid to the difference. The young ones sat alongside the older ones, and surprisingly, they all learned to recite classical verses soon enough, even without much comprehension. Grandfather received his education this way and acquired a lifelong love of poetry and calligraphy.

All those who completed their education and considered themselves scholars would try to pass the four increasingly difficult national examinations offered every three years: the first was local, the next regional, then national; the finalists would take the last exam in front of the Emperor. A person was considered learned if he passed the first exam. He could be commissioned for various prestigious and lucrative civil service jobs if he passed the second and third ones. Passing the final one would make the young man not only famous nationally, but sometimes he would end up marrying one of the Emperor's daughters—if the ruler liked what he saw. I believe Grandfather passed the first level examination and spent his life in leisure as a member of the landed gentry.

My grandmother, a gentle woman known for her kindness to the poor and filial love for her elders, was a fair painter, a self-taught flutist, and Grandfather's peer in writing poetry. In their lucky union, they enjoyed a comfortable living, enriched by their love of literature, poetry, and music. They had four sons and a daughter; only Second Uncle, Third Uncle and Father—the youngest, born in 1899—survived childhood. My grandmother died when Father was in his early teens. Although Grandfather remarried, he always talked about Grandmother in the most loving terms, even fifty years after her death and sometimes in front of his second wife. I still recall the unabashed tears running down his wrinkled cheeks when her name was mentioned.

In the mid-19th century, the last dynasty to rule China—the Qing—was rotting and crumbling under its many domestic problems. It had neither the skill to negotiate with foreign nations nor the military strength to defend its cities. It lost all trade war skirmishes against no less than eight "foreign powers" and signed twenty-one infamous "unequal treaties" in which China ceded land to many and paid heavy indemnity to all. The major coastal cities allowed "foreign enclaves" in which other countries had complete jurisdiction and China was powerless.

Studying the history of that period as junior high students, my classmates and I were incensed at the ineptitude of the Qing. Empress Dowager Cixi used the money meant to rebuild the navy for her own luxurious private garden. We were afire with shame when the inferior Qing army lost one war after another, and calmly accepted the foreigners' terrible terms. Our young eyes burned hot tears when we studied the many unequal treaties that inflicted damage on China for generations to come. From that time on, Western influences—along with warships, missionaries, and superior technology—forced their way into China as it was painfully "opened."

The Hoh family's fate somewhat paralleled that of China. They continued running things as their ancestors had, not willing or able to do differently, but vaguely sensing that the times were changing and their good fortune fading. When money was short, they would sell a little piece of land. Grandfather was aware enough of the changing times to decide to send Third Uncle, a brilliant student, to a "modern" high school in Shanghai, two hundred miles away from home. His curriculum there included mathematics and English. Father later followed Third Uncle's path to Shanghai in 1913.

Third Uncle, having finished his schooling in Shanghai, was attracted to the exciting new ways of Western culture. He studied and worked hard and somehow obtained a scholarship to a French university around 1914. Then he requested Grandfather's permission to go abroad and study, an unheard-of event in Hoh family history. Grandfather was proud and worried at the same time. Besides having to raise the money for the trip, he was also suspicious of what the foreign education might do to his son. Eventually, Grandfather compromised: he would sell some land to pay for the trip, but Third Uncle would have to marry before he left.

Following the custom of the time, Grandfather had arranged a future marriage for my uncle when he was a mere boy, to a young woman of good family. Third Uncle in all likelihood knew nothing of his fiancée and may not have even set eyes on her. Often, before a son left home for any length of time, it was his duty to get married. This act cemented his ties to family and home. Besides, his parents would have the daughter-in-law to serve them in their son's absence. Excited about new ideas and new freedoms in a changing time, Third Uncle was not thrilled at all by the thought of marrying a stranger. But under Grandfather's threat of "no marriage, no foreign education," he reluctantly agreed.

I questioned my father many times about my Third Aunt, but could only conjure up a vague picture of a small woman with ordinary looks, a soft voice, and gentle manners. I imagine that she had some rudimentary education. More importantly, she had the womanly virtues of "patience and obedience" drummed into her from an early age, as did most young women from good families in China at the time. She came to the Hohs to be married to a stranger who was to leave for an unknown land for an indeterminate number of years— the stranger to whom her life would be forever bound. Third Uncle left for France shortly afterwards, and Third Aunt stayed behind to serve her parents-in-law.

Four years later, Third Uncle finished his education and accepted a good job in a bank in Shanghai. He came home to Caodian infrequently. But the folks at home were justifiably proud of him, most of all Grandfather. Third Aunt was probably happy too, now that her husband had finally come back to his own country. She understood that she couldn't accompany him to Shanghai because it was her duty to serve his parents at home.

Things hummed along for a few years until one day Grandfather received a letter from Third Uncle. The walls shook as Grandfather roared. He jumped up and down with rage, slammed his feet on the ground, and pounded his fists on the desk as he yelled curses at Third Uncle. It was some time before the rest of the family could make sense of what he was saying. His unfilial, ungrateful, unprincipled son had written to beg for a divorce! Third Uncle had met and fallen in love with someone in Shanghai, and he wanted to marry her.

Grandfather's terse answer to the letter was unequivocal. He would never allow his son to shame his family with a divorce, unheard of in China at the time.

"Go ahead! Marry that woman and I will hang myself. Let the whole world see how you murder your father. Let that be on your conscience forever."

Since everyone knew that Grandfather didn't make empty threats, no further mention of divorce was heard from Shanghai. Third Uncle came home even less frequently and seemed despondent whenever he did. Grandfather was certain of the righteousness of his decision until the day Third Uncle and his lady-love killed themselves, jumping together into a scenic lake near Shanghai.

Third Uncle's story, for obvious reasons, was rarely talked about in the family. Third Aunt became a non-person afterward. Her status of unwanted wife deteriorated quickly to that of childless widow, with no memories and no hopes—only unending service to her parents-in-law. After Japan invaded China, Grandfather and Step-Grandmother left their home in 1940 to join my parents in Sichuan Province, but Third Aunt was left behind. Father sent money to her for years to maintain her existence. I don't know the details of her later life except that she eventually entered a Buddhist nunnery, a small graying nun praying for her next life in the dark temple.

The unexpected beneficiary of this tragedy was my father. When he reached early manhood and wanted to dissolve his prearranged engagement, Grandfather only half-heartedly threatened to kill himself, and the threat eventually gave way to a reluctant "hao-la, hao-la" ("okay, okay"). Father often said that, if it were not for his brother's tragic death, he might not have married Mother. Then turning to me, he would smile with a twinkle in his eyes and ask, "Then where would you be?"

TWO

Mother's Good Fortune

Mother's family in 1931, from left: Third, Fourth, Fifth, and First Uncles, Grandfather Kao, Second Uncle, Grandmother Kao, Ah Yee, Mother (pregnant with me), and Father. Note the difference between Grandmother's tiny bound feet and Mother's, which are unbound.

M y mother, Tze Kao, was born in 1901 in Nantong, a city
on the Yangzi River in Jiangsu Province. To be born
a girl in China at the turn of the 20th century carried
inherent risks. If she was born into a poor family, she could look
forward to lifelong labor and illiteracy. If her family happened to
be comfortable, she would surely suffer the unspeakable pain of
having her feet bound at five to seven years old. Her crippled feet
wouldn't allow her to ever walk properly again. Tiny feet were
required for marriage to a gentleman whose forefathers no doubt
concocted this cruel practice.

My mother was lucky on many counts. First of all, her family
was comfortably middle-class, and she was the first girl after four
brothers. Even though the Chinese traditionally value male off-
spring much more than female, my grandparents already had the
security of four sons so could enjoy the extravagance of doting on
their first baby girl.

Secondly, her father—my grandfather Kao—was a most unusual
Chinese man. Grandfather had the formal education of a scholar
but later ran the family business. He eventually became president

of the Four Coastal Cities Business Association (a respected chamber of commerce serving millions of residents). Unlike so many of his contemporaries who clung stubbornly to the old ways, Grandfather maintained an open mind to the changing times.

Parents in China were traditionally described as "strict, disciplinary father and gentle, nurturing mother." A Chinese father in Grandfather's time would not show love for his children openly—neither playing with them nor displaying physical affection. His stern mask always stayed in place and only cracked open when he could spoil his grandchildren. In some families, as a sign of respect, the children wouldn't even sit down in their father's presence. If they had any requests of their father, they would ask their mother to relay them. The father was the emperor of his kingdom.

Mother was obviously her father's favorite. Again, she was lucky. She was endowed with a sharp mind, healthy body, and physical beauty—a rare combination at a time when people paid little attention to nutrition and exercise.

Mother grew up surrounded by a loving family. My grandparents and their seven children (another son and daughter were born later) lived in a courtyard house that had been in the Kao family for generations. Typical of that time, the brick house had many living quarters separated by small courtyards. There was enough room to accommodate three generations of the family, relatives who visited for short periods, relatives who were too poor or too infirm to live independently, and servants.

The main courtyard had a pair of impressive doors facing the street. Each door measured eight feet tall and two feet wide, with huge iron door knobs; they were opened only for very important occasions such as holidays, weddings, or funerals. Two small doors on the side served for daily use. Next to the main house, the family owned an incense store and a small factory, where raw incense was processed and packaged. Their few workers lived in the factory as well. Favorites of the children, they would teach them the incense-making process when they were in a good mood and not too busy.

Mother, at the age of five, learned to recite many poems from her favorite cousin who was four years older. The first girls' school had just been established in Nantong to teach elementary reading and writing. Mother's cousin liked going to school, and Mother begged to go, too. The school age for girls at that time was far from standardized. Grandfather appreciated that Mother would be lonely at home without her favorite cousin. He expected her to drop out after a few days but said she could try. So Mother went to Ming Yi Elementary School for Girls at six years old. Surprisingly, she seemed able to learn with the rest of the small class—all girls much older—and enjoyed going to school.

At home, Mother sometimes played with her fourth brother's younger friends. She turned out to be the equivalent of a Chinese tomboy; she ran with the boys and sometimes beat them at their own game. When the boys climbed the tall stone wall near the house, a kind of miniature Great Wall surrounding the city, Mother refused to be left behind. Like the boys, she took off her shoes and stockings so her bare feet could grip the cracks of the wall better. The boys nicknamed Mother "warrior with braids" because, at times, when she worried that her pretty, embroidered shoes might get dirty, she tied them onto her long braids while she climbed.

But when Mother turned seven, Grandmother decided the time had come to have Mother's feet bound so she could learn to be a proper little lady. The practice of foot binding in China had existed for a thousand years. Stories of its origins vary; an emperor is said to have expressed profound admiration for a court dancer's small feet, as shown off by her graceful and fluid steps. Gradually, small feet were imbued with erotic overtones and became the indispensable mark of a woman's beauty. In the upper and middle classes, foot size dictated a girl's marriageability. A bride with a pair of tiny three-inch feet was coveted, as anyone could see that her husband was wealthy enough to allow her to forego manual labor and sit all day long. On the other hand, her luckless sister with five-inch feet could only acquiesce to an inevitably poorer or otherwise less desirable husband.

The atrocious process started when a girl was no older than six or seven. A woman whose sole job was this would closely wrap long strips of cloth around a young girl's feet. The binding was tightened daily. Gradually, over two years, the relentless pressure of the cloth would break the arch and stop the growth of the feet permanently. The excruciating suffering of generations of defenseless young girls was aptly described by the saying, "Every pair of small feet costs a tub of tears."

The pain continued for women with bound feet for the rest of their lives; they suffered poor circulation in their feet and sometimes even gangrene or blood poisoning. Furthermore, none could ever walk for any distance again.

Countless men romanticized women's petite feet, and they were named "golden lotuses." Poets rhapsodized over the graceful, willowy way women with small feet walked. In reality, women whose feet had been bound waddled, especially when they grew old and gained a little weight.

When Mother's time came, she was far from docile and resisted having her feet bound with all her might. She cried, begged, and raged. Ironically, it was the sad responsibility of mothers to ensure that their daughters' feet were bound. Having gone through the torture herself, Grandmother agonized over every wail of her small daughter but had to stand firm. She believed it was her duty as a loving mother to ensure that her daughter's feet were successfully bound so she could marry well.

Being innovative, Mother loosened her bindings at night so she could get a good night's sleep, then tried to put the strips back on in the morning, hoping the foot-binding lady wouldn't notice. Of course, she did and put an end to it by sewing the strips of cloth together. Mother's feet were swollen in no time, and she said they felt as though they were being grilled on a hot skillet. Finally, after about a month of his daughter's suffering and crying, Grandfather could stand it no longer. He unwound all the strips of material from Mother's feet and threw them into the kitchen stove. My grandmother wailed, "Nobody will marry our daughter now!" To which Grandfather answered solemnly, apparently having given the matter serious thought, "That's all right. I'll keep her for as long as I'm able to. She can go to school, become a teacher, and support herself."

As early as the late 18th century, some reform-minded Chinese intellectuals attempted to stop the practice of foot binding, calling it a sign of Chinese backwardness and the cause of frail mothers giving birth to weak children. Governments, both the late Qing and the early Republic, supposedly banned the practice but without strict enforcement. In most of China, it finally ended at the beginning of the twentieth century, a few years after Mother fought with Grandfather's help to escape her crippling fate. But, in some parts of China, the custom lingered on until the late 1920s.

Without the damaging effects of bound feet, Mother grew tall and strong. She became the protector and mentor of her younger brother and sister who adored her. This brother, my Fifth Uncle, often told the story of how he had lost a fight to the older boys in the neighborhood when he was a tyke. He had been reduced to shielding his head with his arms and crouching on the ground. Just when he had given up hope, out of nowhere his sister rushed to his defense and beat back the older boys with a tree branch.

Mother pulled her brother up and bandaged his bleeding knee with a handkerchief. To spare his hurt leg, eight-year-old Mother struggled to carry her five-year-old brother on her back, talking and consoling him while she lumbered toward home. Fifth Uncle couldn't stop sobbing. More than his knee was hurt—the defeat was too much for him.

In desperation, Mother tried something else. She started to curse the bad boys. She racked her brain and used all the limited curse words she could muster, including some she had heard adults using but didn't understand. That did the trick! Fifth Uncle so enjoyed the cursing that he perked up, stopped crying, and joined the game:

Sons of dogs.

No, they're sons of pigs.

They'll fall in the river when they try to cross it.

Yeah, and be eaten by turtles!

They made up endless bad names and painful fates for Uncle's attackers. Brother and sister took turns, admiring each other's creativity and laughing all the way home.

When Mother was fifteen, the marriage broker came. The son of a wealthy family in town sought Mother's hand. It was well known that the young man was a playboy and a stranger to books. Mother suggested to her father that he ask her suitor to write an essay before considering the proposal. My wise grandfather, knowing that his unusual daughter might have a future brighter than that of a rich man's wife, agreed to the scheme and thus turned down the most eligible bachelor in town.

Mother became an athletic star as well as a top student in school. Her teachers began to put ideas in her head that, with all her talents, she should seek higher education in Shanghai, a large city about a hundred miles away. With her teachers' help, Mother secured a scholarship to the YWCA Teachers' College for Women in Shanghai. She started the long campaign to convince her parents to allow her to study there.

Grandmother was strongly against the idea. Who knew what could happen to a young girl, especially one as attractive as Mother, when she was alone in the big city? Mother reassured Grandmother that she wouldn't leave the schoolyard unless her older brother, who worked in Shanghai, accompanied her.

Grandmother was unrelenting and tried to persuade Grandfather to accept her reasoning. Mother fought for her future education with everything in her arsenal, including a hunger strike. She locked herself in her room and refused food for two days. Her parents couldn't bear her suffering so, knowing that their daughter was a serious student, first Grandfather and then Grandmother gave in.

Mother was soon swept up by the excitement of her forthcoming adventure. Her schoolmates, neighbors, and siblings now looked at her with renewed respect, which was only fitting for the first girl to leave town to study in Shanghai. Grandmother realized that her little girl would never live the traditional life of her mother, or her grandmother before her; she was torn between pride and worry.

Grandfather simply said, "I know you will study hard and do the right thing." His love, trust, and understanding in this short sentence went straight to Mother's heart. Grandmother and Mother packed for weeks. After a farewell dinner, Mother left home tearfully with her older brother to start her new life. She was just sixteen.

The Teachers' College was larger and more beautiful than Mother had imagined. It was affiliated with a missionary organization and offered English in the curriculum. Before Mother settled in or had time to assess her environment, a most unexpected thing happened— she was hit by terrible homesickness. Never having been away from home in her life, she was completely overwhelmed by the pain of separation. She missed her parents, her siblings, her schoolmates, and just about everyone else in her hometown. She didn't know how folks at home would get along without her, especially her younger brother and sister. Who would look after them now if they needed help?

Mother couldn't eat, couldn't sleep, and couldn't study. When her older brother came to visit, she was reduced to speechless sobbing. He was so alarmed that he got in touch with their parents. My grandparents became worried, too; their daughter's behavior was most unusual. After three weeks, the news from Mother's college didn't improve. Everyone thought it best for Mother to return home, and she shamefacedly agreed.

Mother's once high spirits seemed broken. She hadn't encountered failure like that before. She was torn with remorse yet felt an overwhelming desire to go home. To herself, she admitted that higher education was now out of reach and resigned herself to teaching at her alma mater in Nantong.

Mother made plans to drop out of college. Grandmother and Mother's younger siblings were delighted. A schoolmate back home even wrote to say that they had saved a spot for her as an alumna at the upcoming school fair, which included a foot race. But a few days before Mother was to leave for home, she received a letter from her father. He scolded her for being so headstrong in her desire to study in Shanghai, then after prevailing, giving in so readily to homesickness. Now that she had made both her parents worry, she might as well come home. Grandfather ended the letter by quoting a well-known Chinese proverb:

"The universe is at peace, but fools make trouble for themselves."

Mother read his letter over and over, shedding many tears. She had to admit that her behavior was exactly like that of the fool in the proverb. In going home now, she would be welcomed with open arms by her loving mother and younger siblings; relatives and friends would also be pleased to see her. But her father? He would be calm as always and taciturn. But she knew in his heart he would be disappointed; he had had faith in her determination to pursue her goal and trusted that she would persevere when faced with adversity. Could she go home now and face his diminished belief in her?

When morning came, she wiped away her tears and realized her father's trust and faith in her were of utmost importance. With gritted teeth, she decided that she would put up with the pain of homesickness to stay and study in Shanghai. She did that for three years, performing so well that her college sent her in 1920 to study in the U.S., first at Mills College in California, and then at the University of Wisconsin in Madison.

Mother was one of the first Chinese women ever to study abroad, and her education became the foundation of her teaching career, which lasted more than seventy years. I can't help but marvel at how different Mother's life would have been had my grandfather not been such an extraordinary man.

THREE

My Young Father

Class photo from Springfield College, 1923

My father, Gunsun Hoh, was born in the town of Caodian, Jiangsu Province, in 1899. He was the youngest of four boys in a landowning family and enjoyed a happy and uneventful childhood. A studious yet active boy, he got into occasional mischief in his teens. A well-remembered highlight was the failed attempt to build a wooden bicycle with his favorite cousin. It looked almost real but couldn't move.

Father lost his mother in his teens, but he never spoke of it. Afterward, he went to study at Ming Li High School in Shanghai in 1913, following the lead of his third brother, who had coached him in English and mathematics. In addition, his father—my grandfather Hoh—had refrained from traveling for a full year to tutor Father in the Chinese classics. This was a major sacrifice as Grandfather loved scenic mountains and lakes and often went on sightseeing trips for months at a time. Father said that having this solid foundation in Chinese served him well for the rest of his life.

Father's name changed from Yen-Jun to Geng-Sheng when he was fifteen, due to an extraordinary incident. The Chinese meaning of "geng sheng" is "born again," although, in my father's case, it had nothing to do with Christianity. On his first summer break from school in Shanghai, Father went to a nearby lake with his younger cousins. They entreated him to show them how to swim as he was wearing "modern" swim trunks from the city.

Not willing to admit that he could barely swim, Father jumped in and splashed around with some "dog paddling" moves. His cousins' applause impelled him to go further and further out until he looked back and realized he couldn't make it back to shore. Once reality set in, he started to sink and swallow water; his young cousins applauded more for his water bubble tricks.

Only a ten-year-old cousin suspected that something was wrong as Father disappeared completely from sight. The boy started yelling, and luckily a father-and-son pair of fishermen was nearby. First, the son got in the water but couldn't find Yen-Jun. The older fisherman knew Grandfather and said, "This is the youngest son of Old Mr. Ninth (Grandfather's nickname as his father's ninth son). We have to find him." He jumped in and succeeded.

The fisherman dragged the unconscious Yen-Jun to land, put him facedown on a big rock and pounded on his back until he threw up water and came to. How he survived in the water, by all accounts for more than twenty minutes, was a lifelong mystery to Father. My traveling grandfather didn't know about the incident until he came home weeks later. He was grateful that Heaven, through the hands of the kind fishermen, had given his son's life back and thus he changed Father's name to "born again." Later, Father anglicized Geng-Sheng to Gunsun.

At the time Father graduated from high school, the Chinese government was encouraging young people to study abroad to learn technology and science from the West. Father wanted to go, so Grandfather did two things for his youngest son—neither of them easy for him. He sold some of the family's precious land to finance the trip. Then, remembering the painful lesson of his third son's suicide, Grandfather reluctantly dissolved the prearranged marriage contract for Father and set him free.

In 1919, Father enrolled at Columbia University in New York, majoring in civil engineering. Once in the U.S., he realized that he didn't have enough money to last him through his studies, so he applied to be a temporary laborer on Sundays. Standing five feet eight inches tall and weighing no more than one hundred forty pounds, he was always rejected. The foreman would look at Father and shake his head, "Too short and too skinny."

Father went back again and again but suffered the same indignity. One beautiful morning, however, the foreman gave Father a small smile and a big shovel and told him to dig. He dug with all his might and got the job. From then on, he worked at whatever part-time jobs he could find to help with his expenses.

One fateful night over dinner, Father got into a heated discussion with his classmate and good friend Zhimo Xu about what China needed most urgently to modernize. Xu, who was to become a well-known poet years later, eloquently presented his case that the physical health of the people was as important as civil engineering, if not more.

Xu pointed out that the Chinese upper class tended to regard physical exercise as something that only poor laborers or martial arts fanatics did. A Chinese ambassador to England once famously asked while watching a tennis match, "Couldn't you hire someone to do the running?" The ideal young male lead in most Chinese operas was portrayed as "full of book learning, pale of face, and without the strength to tie up a chicken."

The idea that there is a connection between a sharp mind and a healthy body was unheard of in China. Xu argued that too many students went abroad to major in civil engineering and too few to study physical education. Father was so completely won over by this argument that, after deliberating, he transferred to Springfield College in Massachusetts for his sophomore year and changed his major to physical education.

Springfield College was then—and still is—a world leader in physical education. Father was a good student, played on the varsity tennis team, and was well liked by his classmates. He formed a lifelong friendship with his roommate, Harry Engleman, who thirty years later became my surrogate father when I came to study in the U.S. Uncle Harry told me how my father loved to dive onto his roommate's bed for fun as soon as he walked into their room. His friends, who not surprisingly had nicknamed him "Son of a Gun" or "H2O," quickly put an end to this practice when they hid layers of hardback books under the bed cover.

Back in China after graduation, Father taught at universities in Wuhan and Suzhou before moving to renowned Qinghua University in Beijing, where he met Mother in 1927. Two years later, they married, and he was made Director of Physical Education at Northeastern University in Shenyang, Manchuria. Shortly afterward, the university had to relocate to Beijing abruptly when Japan invaded Manchuria in a surprise attack.

Father organized the retreat of the university, arranging transportation for the students and later lodging and classrooms for them. He continued to teach in Beijing until, in 1933, he was offered a position at the National Ministry of Education in Nanjing, overseeing physical education for all youth in China. Father held that position with the Nationalist government for the next thirty-seven years, dedicating his whole life to realizing his friend Xu's vision.

FOUR

My Parents' Love Story

My parents' wedding portrait, Beijing 1929.

My parents were born at the turn of the 20th century in a China undergoing turbulent change. Over the previous seventy years, the crumbling Qing Dynasty had been shaken out of its isolation and repeatedly defeated by foreign aggressors. The Chinese finally saw the painful truth—their country was not only inferior in military strength but also backward in technology and education.

In 1912, the Qing Dynasty was overthrown, and the Republic of China established. Many intellectuals realized the need for reform, and the newly formed government devised plans to send students abroad to study and learn from the Western industrialized countries.

My parents were lucky to be among the first to have that opportunity. When my mother decided to major in physical education at the University of Wisconsin, the field was unknown in China and qualified teachers of physical education were nonexistent. The prevailing sentiment about women's education could then be summed up by the saying, "Women without talents are virtuous." They could be allowed to learn writing and reading, but their first obligation was to learn the women's virtues: patience, obedience, self-sacrifice, etc.

Against such a cultural background, I am all the more amazed by my enlightened Grandfather Kao, who let my mother study in a foreign country and willingly put up half of the expenses as required by the college. Tze was determined to make her father proud. Having lived away from home in Shanghai for two years, she had gained a handle on her homesickness and quickly adjusted to the foreign environment; she knew not to ask for ice cream at breakfast anymore. She was quickly swept up in the excitement of learning something new every day, including nutrition, hygiene, and even anatomy alongside medical students. A good student and a natural athlete who was five foot six—unusually tall for a Chinese woman at that time—she even played on the women's varsity basketball team.

In 1923, my father and mother each returned to China and began their respective teaching careers. Two years later, both changed jobs and moved to teach in Beijing, which, with its six universities, was renowned as a center of education. Having been the capital of numerous dynasties, Beijing was one of the loveliest and most cultured old cities in China. Many of its majestic palaces, grand temples, and beautiful gardens and lakes, once restricted to royalty, could now be visited by everyone. The city was known for its gourmet restaurants as well as street vendors, offering delicious food for the wealthy and common folk alike. Chinese opera and traditional folk arts, such as storytelling and acrobatics, reached their pinnacle in this center of culture.

My mother, Tze, was only twenty-four when she was named chair of the Physical Education and Health Science Department in the newly formed Women Teachers' College. Not much older than her students, Tze was much loved by them. After my mother died at ninety-six, one of her earliest students, Lucy Lu, wrote an article paying tribute to her as "Teacher of Teachers." These are some excerpts from it:

On the first day of school, Teacher Kao gave us a physical examination [probably just weight, height, eyesight, etc.]. *She was kind and caring, more so than any other teacher I had ever had. I was wearing a pair of fashionable shoes, and Teacher Kao said gently, "It's best not to wear shoes with pointed toes; they might deform your feet." From that day onward, whenever she saw me in the morning, she would call me by my name and say good morning. I was flattered that she should remember my name after that short encounter. Then I found out that she did that with all the students! We were amazed by her phenomenal memory.*

She gave the best lectures. She worked tirelessly to teach us hygiene, nutrition, basketball, volleyball, etc. She was ever ready to help us whether we had difficulty in school or our personal lives.

She drew attention wherever she went, not just because of her height, but her lovely face and gracious manner. She treated us like younger sisters and friends, and we all fell in love with Teacher Kao.

Although it might seem strange now to think of women students "falling in love" with a woman teacher, this was actually quite common in China in the 1920s. Still living under the veil of traditional customs, college girls would never admit to being infatuated with a male teacher, nor openly talk about a boyfriend, if by rare chance they had one. However, it was permissible to be infatuated with a woman teacher and talk endlessly about her:

We were the silly kids who adored Teacher Kao. Although we all tried to take her courses, not everyone had Teacher Kao as lecturer. If one of us saw her in the morning and said hello to her, she would report that chance meeting to the other girls and that "sighting" would keep her happy all day.

Now, seventy long years later, looking back as an old woman myself, I can still clearly see Teacher Kao in her splendor, standing there lovely and straight. My pure love for her is forever linked to all the sweetness and innocence of my youth and the happy school days which were soon to be cut short by the war.

My father, Gunsun, taught at the well-known Qinghua University, also in Beijing. Energetic and enthusiastic, he headed a core group of young teachers promoting physical education and became the first president of the Association for the Advancement of Physical Education. Of its two vice presidents, one was a man, and the other was the new teacher from the Women Teachers' College—Tze Kao.

Gunsun had opportunities to see Tze often, and they had much to talk about. They shared a commitment to teaching, and both loved sports. They appreciated having had the privilege of a good education and were passionate about making good use of it. They were young, full of energy, optimistic about their future, and excited about the changes they knew they were bringing to their young students' lives. They were often seen riding their bicycles on the wide, willow-lined avenue near Tze's school or other scenic places. Before long, they fell in love.

Of the many happy memories of my childhood, I most enjoyed hearing my father talk about his courtship of Mother. During the late 1930s, in the midst of the Sino-Japanese War (1937–1945), my family lived without electricity or running water in a rural village near Chongqing. On hot summer nights, we tried to escape the heat by gathering outdoors on the porch. While we fanned ourselves and ate watermelon in the evening, Father needed little encouragement to tell stories. Sometimes Mother and my aunt would laughingly fill in the footnotes.

Father began, "You know, Mother had many admirers. Oh, I would say one university president and two professors for sure. Others were undeclared candidates who turned red and stammered whenever she was within sight. I often felt like I had to fight off a whole army of competitors. Thanks to the Association for the Advancement of Physical Education, I had more chances to be with her than the others. I believe the Association was the 'red string' that tied our feet together."

A popular Chinese folktale tells of "The Old Man Under the Moon," a love god who ties a red string between the feet of a future couple. No matter how far apart they are initially, the red string eventually brings them together to meet and marry.

Father continued, "My university was more than ten miles away from Mother's college. I tried to see her every day after work. Bicycling would have been easier on my wallet, but it took up too much precious time. How I ran up a mountain of taxi fares!"

Throughout his life, Gunsun was overly generous and never paid much attention to money. Before his marriage, as a well-compensated college professor with nobody to support but himself, he somehow managed to be frequently broke. Tze, on the contrary, was always careful with money. Nevertheless, she was happily overwhelmed when she came home from work one day to find that the florist had delivered twenty pots of yellow chrysanthemums to her small apartment—from a Mr. Hoh.

"What a crazy man your father was!" Mother recalled. "There were chrysanthemums in the living room, study, on the porch…."

"Mother, Mother, did you fall in love with Father after that?" I asked excitedly.

"Well, I liked him a lot. Working with him in the Association, I came to see his dedication and courage, and I admired that, but you know what bothered me a little?"

"What?"

"That your father was only a little more than an inch taller than me."

"I beg your pardon," Father countered, faking indignation, "one-and-three-quarters inches, to be exact."

"What silly things bother young girls," Mother laughed. "Now, I wouldn't mind if Father were a foot shorter!"

"You know when I really fell in love with Mother?" Father liked to tell his side of the story.

"Of course I know! The first day you saw Mother. You've told me many times."

"True, I was smitten the first time I met her. But I really, really fell in love with Mother after she fell off her bicycle."

"What happened?"

"We were out riding one day. Mother's bicycle hit a stone, and she went flying to the ground. I jumped down to check the damage and was aghast to see blood gushing from her hands and knee. Her knee was so deeply cut I could even see the whitish tendon. Yet Mother remained cool. She bit her lip but didn't cry or moan. We couldn't find a taxi and finally got a rickshaw to take her to the hospital. Mother waited patiently, and she was her same gracious self when she talked to the doctor. I was most impressed." For a moment Father was lost in his memory of that long-ago day; he nodded his head almost imperceptibly with a proud little smile.

Even though arranged marriage was still the norm, Gunsun and Tze were lucky to have parents who respected their children's wishes. Gunsun's father had long ago given his son the freedom to make his own match. Tze idolized her dignified and reserved father, yet he was also an enlightened liberal at heart. He had allowed his favorite daughter to be the first to leave her hometown to study in Shanghai and, later, the U.S. It seemed only natural that he would allow her to choose her own mate. Nevertheless, when old Mr. Kao visited his daughter in Beijing, Gunsun was flustered.

Grandfather Kao was a connoisseur of Chinese opera and had bought expensive tickets to an opera sung by a nationally renowned actor. He invited his daughter and her special friend to accompany him. Gunsun was, of course, anxious to make a good impression on the father of the woman he loved, so he tried desperately to hide the fact that he was neither interested in nor knew anything about Chinese opera. He had even read up on the actor beforehand so he could converse about him intelligently. My aunt Ah Yee, Mother's baby sister, a high school student in Beijing at the time, was also in the party. She described the meeting like this:

"Everything went smoothly during the dinner and the first half of the opera. During intermission, it was common custom for the waiters to serve hot towels to the patrons. After the guests wiped their faces and hands, the waiters would collect the soiled towels. To save time, the waiters on the balcony level had developed a routine of throwing the used towels all the way across the theater to one waiter in the far corner to take them away."

"We were sitting on the first floor, and the towels were flying over our heads. The audience was used to this routine, and nobody paid much attention. Only your father was fascinated. He craned his neck this way and that to look at the towels flying. I caught my father's strange look when your father committed the unthinkable by applauding the waiters."

Father laughed, "Well, I had never been to a high-class opera before nor seen such towel throwing. To throw a wet towel across such distance and with such precision! I couldn't help but be impressed. Good thing my future father-in-law didn't make opera-going a prerequisite for his daughter's hand."

My grandmother Kao liked Gunsun right away. He was respectful to her, yet warm and playful. He would even joke with her, something none of her five sons ever did, and she secretly enjoyed it. Soon both Tze's parents gave their blessing for the engagement.

My aunt Ah Yee loved to tell another anecdote that my father often conveniently forgot:

"Your father was always sweet to Grandma. After your parents were engaged, one day Grandpa and Mother went somewhere, and your father decided to take Grandma and me to lunch. We went to North Sea—a scenic lake—walked around the water, then went to a restaurant and ordered their signature fried noodles. He was telling Grandma some funny story and had her laughing and giggling. Then the noodles came on a big plate. Your father was in a jovial mood, and he suddenly asked, 'Do you want to see me do an arm-twisting trick?' We said, 'Sure, sure. Show us.'"

"Your father picked up the plate of noodles." My aunt got up to demonstrate how the "trick" was done. "He put it on his right hand then spun his wrist, moving it first under his right arm, then over his head in a big arc. All the time he tried to keep the plate upright and level. He was moving gracefully like a Thai dancer doing a candle dance, and we were applauding loudly. Then, all of a sudden, BAM! He lost his balance and the plate, along with our lunch, crashed to the ground. He turned bright red. He ran to ask the waiter to clean up the mess and put in another rush order. Grandma was thoroughly amused, but Father apologized all over the place and begged us not to tell Mother. Of course, I couldn't wait to tell her! I don't think Father ever lived it down."

Apparently, Gunsun's blunders, or his "near misses" as he called them, did no lasting damage, and Tze's parents announced their wedding a year later.

I was amused by Lucy Lu's account of how my mother's students took the news:

> *Someone found out that Teacher Kao was to marry Gunsun Hoh. Not able to feel the least bit happy for her, on the contrary, we were disappointed and grief-stricken. Teacher Kao was perfection in our eyes and we wanted her to remain the subject of our love always. And if she should marry one day, her intended had to be handsome as Liu Lan [a movie star] and talented as Li Bo [a celebrated poet]. In our eyes, Gunsun Hoh was neither. How could she lower herself to marry him?*

Tze and Gunsun had a large wedding. They wanted a simple and dignified ceremony and put much thought into its planning. They decided to do away with the usual overlong speeches by family and friends. Another tradition was for guests to compose congratulatory poems or verses as gifts to the newlyweds. They were then written on red silk banners and hung in the wedding hall. In large numbers, though, the banners could be overwhelming. So the young couple politely told their friends that they would treasure the red banners but not hang them at the ceremony.

My father reminisced, "We had given detailed instructions for how the wedding hall was to be decorated. As I was nervously finishing dressing, I thought I had better have a last look at the hall before the guests arrived. Imagine my shock when I saw a huge red banner hanging on the center wall that said:

Two experts in physical education,
Two physical bodies combine into one,
One big event of getting married,
You are allowed to marry but not divorce.

"Those lines were meant to be naughty jokes. The talk about two physical bodies combining was definitely risqué for Chinese society at that time, and the mention of 'divorce' was pure taboo."

Father continued, "Now the jokes and pranks I had played on my friends came back to plague me! I was angry at my friends who were getting back at me at this crucial moment. What's more, I was scared that my future father-in-law would walk in at any minute and surely be offended. I barely had time to remove the banner before he arrived. Fortunately, the ceremony went smoothly after this incident."

After they married, Gunsun and Tze both continued their teaching careers. They had an idyllic life—professions they enjoyed and friends, co-workers, and students who cared about them. A year later, Gunsun accepted an offer to head the Department of Physical Education at the renowned Northeastern University in Shenyang, Manchuria.

Tze decided to resign her job in order to move with him. That set off a tearful and irate protest from her students. Despite Tze's patient and gentle explanation of her commitment as a wife, the students were inconsolable. Gunsun received an invitation for tea from Tze's students, and he went with thoughts of somehow mollifying them:

"When I arrived, I was surprised that your mother was not there. The students made no move to wait for her; it turned out that they had schemed to invite only me. One after another, they got up to give speeches: one pleading with tears running down her face, another arguing with cold anger. They understood that Mother had a commitment to me, but they in the graduating class needed her just as much. Their desperate tears embarrassed me and their heated arguments confused me. I was deeply moved by their devotion to Mother, and I began to think that maybe I was being selfish to take Mother away. Eventually, the students extracted a promise from me to do my best to help."

The outcome of this demonstration was that, after much discussion, Tze consented to delay her move. She joined Gunsun at Northeastern University a year later.

The year was 1930. My parent's first home was a beautiful one with redwood furniture, a wedding present from Tze's parents. Gunsun had teaching as well as administrative responsibilities, which he greatly enjoyed. Tze also taught at the University. A year later, they were delighted to learn that Tze was pregnant with their first child—me. No one knew that within the year Japan was to invade Manchuria the same way it did Pearl Harbor a decade later, i.e. without provocation, without declaration of war. Gunsun and Tze's world would be shattered—a piece of fragile Chinese jade crushed by an iron hammer.

My parents' lives would never be the same. From that moment on, they started an exodus that would last fifteen years—running, dodging, trying to stay ahead of the invading Japanese army—never knowing when the next move would be necessary.

Altogether, my parents moved eleven times due to the war. They lost all their possessions. They were bombed and shot at. Gunsun was almost killed by shrapnel, and Tze lost a pregnancy while carrying Gunsun to and from the air raid shelter. They continued to teach and work throughout, sometimes in lecture halls housed in temporary buildings and temples. They never lost the conviction that they were making a difference for their young students. We were lucky to come out of the war alive and together.

Despite all their hardships, my parents' marriage was one of the happiest that I know of—a lifelong love affair with shared values, similar goals, and complementary personalities. That didn't mean that they didn't fight. In fact, with two quick tempers and strong wills, they had some fights that scared Ah Yee and me to tears. But they agreed on a golden rule early in their marriage—no fight would last overnight. Somehow they managed to talk and make up before the night was over.

I would venture to say that it was mostly my father who made the first move, but Mother also responded graciously, never one to pout or hold grudges. I remember one time after a spectacular fight and makeup, they decided to celebrate the joy of reunion by going away for the weekend. They actually took me out of school so I missed my Saturday classes. I didn't care, only too happy to feel the sunshine after the storm.

My parents were well known in the circles of education and physical education. My mother was elegant, well-spoken and dignified. Rumor had it, however, that my father was "afraid of his wife." On the fortieth anniversary of their marriage, Father wrote a short article for the newspaper on being a "hen-pecked" husband.

As for men everywhere, being called hen-pecked was meant to be a real insult. But my father said he was proud to be one, with the qualification that he listened to my mother not out of fear but genuine respect and admiration for her opinion. Listening to her counsel and following her advice for forty years had worked out well for him. He enumerated my mother's outstanding qualities and then asked the question, "If you had a wife like mine, wouldn't you do what I have done for these forty years?"

To my occasional embarrassment, Father couldn't encounter a single man, whether a new friend or an unknown waiter, without asking, "Are you married? Why not? Being married is a lot better than being single."

When my son Duncan was a toddler, Father came to visit me alone on one of his work trips. I was ironing, and Father sat on a sofa facing me. We talked about everything: Chinese news, world news, neighbors, and of course everyone at home. Then, he suddenly asked, "Do you think there is life after death?" I answered carelessly and flippantly, as only the young would, "Nah, when you die, there is nothing." I then kicked myself black and blue for being insensitive and thoughtless when I looked up and saw tears on Father's face. I rushed over to hug him. He looked up at me, still unable to stop crying, and said, "I couldn't bear it if one day I couldn't see Mother."

There was so much love in their long marriage. I am grateful they were my parents.

FIVE

Ah Yee

Ah Yee in Taiwan circa 1960

My mother's baby sister, Yen Kao, whom I called Ah Yee in Chinese, was born in 1909 and was one of the last victims of smallpox in China. The virus infected her when she was an infant, still nursing at her mother's breast. Even though she escaped with her life, the disease left her completely disfigured: pea-sized pockmarks covered her face and body like so many little craters, the bridge of her nose collapsed, and her lips looked thick and swollen for the rest of her life. My grandmother also developed a mild infection that left pockmarks around her nipples. The children in the family, including my mother and her younger brother, were sent away so they could escape the debilitating grip of the disease. Sadly, an older cousin who stayed to help care for Yen contracted the disease and died from it.

Ah Yee was a gorgeous baby before smallpox struck, but she was doomed to be physically ugly thereafter. (In her fifties, she had many cosmetic operations, which improved her appearance a great deal.) As a child, I didn't pay much attention to my aunt's looks. To me, she was always Ah Yee, the aunt who loved me and the aunt who yelled at me. As I grew older, I understood how difficult it must have been for Ah Yee to grow up as a child and to live as a young woman with a face like hers. I shudder to imagine the startled looks from people when they first laid eyes on her, the cruel jokes of children, and the unbearable pity from those who didn't know her.

Having a scarred face was especially hard since quite a few members of the Kao family were noted for their good looks. For example, my cousin De was a well-known beauty in her college days and only a few years younger than Ah Yee; they even shared the same circle of friends. Ah Yee told me once, quite dispassionately, that when she and De were together, she always sent De to ask for directions or other help from strangers. De got much better results than she could have.

Ah Yee lived with my parents from the time they got married. When I was growing up, there were always the three of them: Father, Mother, and Ah Yee. Eight years younger than Mother, Ah Yee was not quite my second mother; she seemed much younger and bubblier. She also had many "juvenile" habits: she liked to eat sweets, sleep late, and read junk "Chinese Westerns."

For close-knit sisters, Mother and Ah Yee were different in looks, temperament, and habits; they were like two people from opposite sides of a vast ocean, connected only by a bridge of love. Mother was tall; Ah Yee short. Mother was hardworking, a perfectionist, and always gave one hundred percent; Ah Yee was an artist at cutting corners.

Both my parents were conscientious in doing exercises every day; no amount of effort could persuade Ah Yee to join them on their daily walk. If there was anything said to be good for health, Ah Yee would buy it for Mother and Father, but she didn't bother to take care of her own health. She could never remember to take her vitamins unless Mother put them in her hands. Ah Yee said that she was in top shape and didn't need to bother with vitamins.

Mother was well organized, a superb teacher and administrator. Ah Yee was never known to make a "to do" list. She relied on her splendid memory to help her on all occasions. If Mother hadn't put Ah Yee's winter clothes away, her heavy pajamas might have stayed on the back of the chair until the next winter.

Mother wrote weekly letters to me for forty years until her hands were too unsteady to continue. In the same period, Ah Yee might have written me ten letters. She saw no need to write since Mother had reported all the news. Mother had various interests: she grew orchids, raised chickens, and took lessons in Chinese painting and singing Chinese opera. Ah Yee's only interest besides reading was playing mah-jongg.

A natural dancer, Ah Yee majored in dance in college. Although she didn't have a dancer's lithe body, she was all grace and fluidity when she danced—an amazing transformation. In 1942 Ah Yee and a musician colleague were the first to travel to northwest China including Tibet, to conduct a systematic study of the folk dances and music of many minority tribes. At that time, travel was hard and accommodations primitive. However, Ah Yee could be fearless when she was determined. She persevered and spent three months on her study trip. In 1954, she went on another field trip to the mountains in Taiwan and documented the music and dances of Taiwan's aborigines. With riches like that, she published many writings on Chinese folk dances and rightfully claimed the title of "Mother of Chinese Folk Dance."

In addition, Ah Yee and Mother probed records of ancient Chinese dances performed at court. Based on these, they choreographed four representative Chinese dances, still taught and performed in Taiwan schools today.

She taught dance in many schools for more than sixty years, finishing her career as founder and chair of the dance department of the Chinese Culture University. Father said that Ah Yee had the "devil's talent," meaning that when it was absolutely necessary, Ah Yee could work very hard and come through with flying colors. This was true; she took her students to perform Chinese folk dances all over the world in cultural exchange programs and made a success of it.

There always seemed to be two sides to Ah Yee: one for peacetime, one for crisis. When things were calm at home, she showed no interest in anything domestic and would read or lounge around after work. But if a family crisis arose, Ah Yee would spring into action and go without sleep for days. Whenever I was sick, Mother and Ah Yee would work together to nurse me. Ah Yee would take the night shift, insisting that Mother get some sleep. It was always Ah Yee's habit to do the heavy lifting to lighten Mother's burden.

Ah Yee's relationships with the family had multiple sides, too. I don't believe she ever said a harsh word to Mother in her whole life. To my father, she was mostly a loving younger sister-in-law, but she was not above making fun of Father's various habits, occasionally criticizing or mocking him. Her relationships with her nephews and nieces, however, were another matter. Ah Yee faithfully practiced the outdated Chinese belief that younger members of the family existed to serve and obey their elders. And the older folks, who had natural wisdom, could correct or scold the children at will.

She believed that young people should never talk back, even if wrongly accused. In my teens, there were various cousins studying near us, away from their hometowns. They were constantly running in and out of our house on weekends or vacations. Ah Yee treated them all equally—she yelled at whoever displeased her at that moment with her special brand of cutting sarcasm:

"Where's the book that I told you to get for me from Mr. Lee?"

"Oh…I forgot…I have to finish my book report, which is due tomorrow."

"You forgot? Why didn't you say anything about the report? Poor Mr. Lee didn't forget and waited at home all morning. What's wrong with your memory? Getting senile before your time, eh? Go get it this afternoon."

"Ah…you told me to take Cousin Jian [who had just come from the country] to a movie."

"Ha! Movies you wouldn't forget, would you?" She then threw up both her arms. "Alibis, alibis. Always from you come the alibis."

Ah Yee actually used the English word "alibi," by which she meant excuses. She had picked it up somewhere, fell in love with it, and used it on us whenever she had a chance.

Ah Yee would lavish money and care on her many nieces and nephews but had no reservations about yelling at us for some insignificant infraction the next moment. At times, it seemed that hunting season was open and we young cousins couldn't run out of her sight fast enough. People said she was just showing an old maid's temper. Yet even when I was a young teenager, I knew that her bark was worse than her bite; behind all that yelling, Ah Yee had a soft heart for all of us.

As Ah Yee grew older, she became mellower, and some of her feistiness left her. At times I almost missed her sarcasm. After Mother had retired as the head of the Teachers' In-Service Training Center in Taiwan, she was given the use of the center's old automobile. She hired "Old He" as her chauffeur.

Old He was a retired army man who could only drive a car slightly faster than walking and thus commanded a salary much less than the going rate. Mother didn't mind his lack of speed. In the horrendous traffic of Taibei, knowing that Old He was going too slowly to hit anybody, Mother could relax in the car. Old He loved to pontificate and often inserted himself in his passengers' conversations. This bad habit and his poor memory of directions irritated Ah Yee to no end.

At one busy intersection, five roads came together at a roundabout with a statue of General Sun in the center. This circle often confused Old He, and one night he made the wrong turn again. He waved his hand wildly to excuse his mistake and said:

"I always turn onto the right road in the daytime. I can tell the roads by the direction General Sun is facing. Now, in the dark, I can't see him so clearly...."

Ah Yee retorted, "So it's not your fault at all. Maybe we could raise money to buy a white smock for General Sun to wear, so General He can see General Sun clearly at night."

My interactions with Ah Yee seemed to have three distinct phases. When I was a young child, Ah Yee was the kind caregiver, nursing me through more than one serious illness. During my teenage years, all I remember is Ah Yee scolding me sarcastically, supposedly correcting my various bad habits for my own good: not standing straight, not doing what I was told, biting my lips when I was nervous, and— the worst offense—talking back.

Finally, during the last forty-some years of her life, while I lived in the U.S. and visited home infrequently, Ah Yee treated me like an equal, often with the thoughtfulness and consideration she reserved for Mother and Father.

I remember that, when my husband died tragically in an accident in Taiwan in 1970, Ah Yee instantly offered to take a leave of absence from her teaching position to help me out in the U.S. It turned out that my mother-in-law and I were able to manage without Ah Yee's help, but I never forgot her sincere and unselfish offer, made on the spot, without any thought of her own sacrifice.

Ah Yee had a special relationship with my brother Hsiang, nine years my junior. She spoiled him rotten. She doted on him from the time he was a darling-looking baby and continued to do so throughout his life. She could never say no to him.

Hsiang was nine when I left home to study in the States. From Mother's weekly letters over forty years, I learned about his turbulent teenage years, his barely graduating from high school, and his two marriages and many disastrous love affairs. He managed to give all three elders terrible headaches. Ah Yee yelled at him no less than at her other nephews, yet never failed to protect him or bail him out of trouble.

Throughout her long teaching career, Ah Yee commingled her substantial income with my parents' funds. Money never meant much to Ah Yee, who took over the family finances after we moved to Taiwan in 1949. She got the job by default because, with their busy professional lives, my parents had neither the interest nor time to deal with it.

Ah Yee was not a good money manager; she had no budget and kept track of expenses sporadically. It was my family's good fortune that Taiwan's economy flourished over the next fifty years. Their combined salaries and later, pensions, grew yearly and afforded them a comfortable lifestyle, despite Ah Yee's haphazard money management.

As the family's accountant, Ah Yee carried a great big pocketbook that was nicknamed the "Hundred Treasures Trunk." I took pleasure in searching for the biggest pocketbook I could find in the U.S. and supplying it to Ah Yee. Her pocketbook always seemed to me a garage waiting for a yard sale. One could find money tucked away in various pockets, usually quite a bit but exactly what amount, Ah Yee never bothered to count. One might also find nail scissors, a hairbrush, cookies, a book, pieces of clothing, movie ticket stubs, and dance recital programs from two years before.

Ah Yee had a mind like a steel trap that she used to remember important things and trivia alike. She easily kept in her head phone numbers for friends and family, her favorite restaurants, hairdresser, taxi companies, etc. Without a pocket calendar, she seemed to remember all her appointments.

Ah Yee was essential for our family fun; she knew which new restaurant was good and what movie or Chinese opera was the rage. She could direct us to small, interesting restaurants in the labyrinth of Taibei's back streets and alleys. More importantly, we depended upon Ah Yee to order the special dishes in each restaurant. A family outing without Ah Yee lacked spontaneity and sparkle—it just didn't seem fun without her!

Father died in 1975 when Mother was in her seventies, and she was inconsolable. Ah Yee became Mother's rescuer. She slept in the same bed with Mother so she could wake her from the occasional nightmare. Ah Yee accompanied Mother wherever she went so she didn't have to hail a taxi in Taibei's congested streets after Old He retired. Ah Yee looked after Mother in every daily task until Mother was strong enough to go back to her beloved teaching, giving her another twenty years of a productive career. When Mother's health declined in her nineties, Ah Yee gladly took up the brunt of caregiving for Mother, even though she was in her eighties herself. By the time Mother died at the age of ninety-six, the two sisters had lived together for more than eighty years.

The decline of Mother's health was slow but inexorable and very painful for me to witness. I increased my visits to Taiwan. The bittersweetness of those times remains etched in my mind. My emotions were a jumbled mess—I was distraught over Mother's hopeless condition, anxious to make every minute count, and guilty that I couldn't be there more.

Because of Mother's frailty, we stayed home a lot. One night we were given tickets to a rare performance by a Chinese opera troupe from Beijing. Mother wisely predicted that getting a taxi afterward would be difficult and decided not to go. So Ah Yee and I went. The troupe lived up to its reputation and more; the singing and acting were superb, the composer made ingenious puns, and the result was clever and at times hilarious. The performers had the audience laughing, howling, and crying at the same time. Ah Yee and I kept saying to each other, "Oh, if only Mother had come with us."

After the show, a summer storm raged outside. Sure enough, we waited half an hour but failed to get a taxi or even get near a bus. Ah Yee remembered there was a long-distance bus stop two blocks away and thought it might be easier for us to catch that. Dripping wet even with our umbrellas, we sloshed through the mud and water and finally caught that bus after a little wait. While we were shivering in our wet clothes, we sang a different tune and kept repeating to each other, "Thank goodness Mother didn't come."

We eventually got off the bus in a less congested area, hailed a taxi, and got home after one a.m. Mother had waited worriedly in the living room for hours. Her eyes lit up, and a big smile broke out when she saw us. With outstretched arms, she said, "Oh, you angels from heaven!"

Ah Yee and I took hot showers and devoured the leftovers Mother had warmed up for us. We described the opera and our odyssey to

Mother with great excitement, interrupting each other to fill in the details. Basking in her relief and joy at seeing us safely home, Mother listened, laughed, and made jokes. That night remained a bright spot in my memory of those gray days of Mother's decline. It was as if time had rolled back and Mother and Ah Yee were young again.

Mother lingered near the end for more than a year, and Ah Yee endured the physical and emotional hardship of caring for her. Even with the help of a nurse, it was Ah Yee who comforted Mother when she couldn't sleep at night. It was Ah Yee who accompanied Mother to doctors' visits. After being told that little more could be done for Mother, Ah Yee kept smiling and tried to cheer her sister up. Watching Mother wasting away before my eyes, I couldn't help being depressed, but Ah Yee was made of tougher stuff. Often after Mother had finally fallen asleep, Ah Yee and I tiptoed out of the bedroom and sat down to have a cup of tea together.

"Ah Yee, I'm so sorry I'm not more help to you," I would often say.

She answered matter-of-factly: "You know I'd do anything for Mother. Don't you fret. You take care of your mother-in-law in the U.S., and I'll look after Mother. I just want to do all I can and not have any regrets after she's gone."

When Mother died, the curtain fell on Ah Yee's life as well. Her lifelong companion, her support, her counsel, and her confidante had been taken away. Her loss was heartbreaking because she had never really been apart from Mother. She gradually lost interest in everything, even her favorite mah-jongg game.

After Mother died, Ah Yee bought a condominium where she lived with Hsiang and his family. During my weekly phone calls, she always said she was fine, sounding as if she were resigned to her fate and patiently waiting for the end. I think that was the beginning of her dementia even though she didn't show any obvious symptoms until much later. It was as if she just didn't see the point of using her sharp mind anymore.

I missed Ah Yee's funeral in 2001 because my flight to Taiwan was scheduled for the day after 9/11 and was canceled. All that day, I sat by myself quietly, and images of Ah Yee ran through my mind: laughing, eating, dancing, scolding, playing mah-jongg, giving, giving, and giving. The most lasting was a back view of Ah Yee in her red raincoat climbing a set of stairs in 1996. On that visit, I only found out at the Taiwan airport that I didn't have an "exit permit" required for visitors who had stayed for more than two months. I went to the police station to apply for one. Ah Yee insisted on accompanying me despite my protest, saying, "You've become an American, and you don't know how things are done in Taiwan anymore. I'd better go with you."

We spent a whole day at the police station, hand delivering the documents from one office to another, and climbing stairs in between. Ah Yee no longer had her dancer's light-footed grace, and the stairs were difficult for her. On that cold day, she wore her favorite red raincoat, which looked swollen because of the heavy sweater underneath. She didn't want me to help her, saying it was easier for her to hold the handrails. I carried her "Hundred Treasures Trunk" on my shoulder and followed behind. A little shaky on her feet, she struggled to pull herself up the stairs, resting every few minutes. Not forgetting to give me a small reassuring smile that said, "I'm all right," she soon resumed her struggle and pulled on the handrail again. That image went straight to my heart. To her loved ones, Ah Yee's gallantry knew no bounds.

SIX

A Young Widow in China

Ven-Long Yin and Yue-Fang Sun's wedding portrait, Shanghai 1929

My mother-in-law was born in 1906 in Shanghai. Her given name was Yue-Fang, meaning "Fragrant Moon." The Sun family was well-to-do, but her parents believed that daughters needed only to learn enough reading, writing, and arithmetic to manage a family. When she finished the equivalent of junior high school, her father thought that she should stay home and help her sickly mother to run their household. Yue-Fang wanted badly to study three more years, but her father's refusal was firm. As an obedient daughter, she eventually acquiesced.

Throughout her life, Yue-Fang blamed herself for not fighting harder for her education and rued her father's unfairness in forcing her to run his household because she was much more capable than her own mother.

The families of both Yue-Fang Sun and her future husband, Ven-Long Yin, were in business in Shanghai and moved in the same social circles. In fact, Yue-Fang went to a girl's school with the Yin sisters, and Yue-Fang's brother was a classmate of Ven-Long's. The Yin family matriarch had seen Yue-Fang at some social gathering and liked her immediately. The old lady had wanted Yue-Fang as a wife for her favorite son, Ven-Long, from that moment on but Yue-Fang's father, Grandfather Sun, had some reservations about the marriage proposal.

Like many Chinese families at that time, the Yin family was a large one, consisting of the matriarch Grandmother Yin, her two married sons with their families, the unmarried Ven-Long, and two unmarried daughters. Sixty-some family members, counting the servants, all lived together in a huge house. Grandfather Sun worried that his daughter might have difficulty adjusting to such a complicated household but eventually agreed to the engagement, which was formalized by a prenuptial ceremony.

Shanghai in the 1920s was in the grip of change, shedding some of its old Chinese ways in favor of new Western ones. Once they became engaged, the bride- and groom-to-be were allowed to get to know one another.

Ven-Long came to the Sun house soon afterward, escorted by Yue-Fang's brother and obviously intending to see her. She spotted them in the hallway and did a quick turnabout and ran upstairs to her bedroom, face flushed and heart pounding. Several days later, the resourceful Ven-Long had his sister call Yue-Fang on the telephone; when she answered, he took the receiver and inquired, "Why didn't you want to speak to me?" So that was the first sentence my father-in-law ever spoke to my mother-in-law. Later, Yue-Fang softened and went to the movies with her intended.

Ven-Long was an up-and-coming young businessman, and he was totally enchanted with Yue-Fang. He also impressed her favorably because, like her, he was interested in learning. Ven-Long even promised to hire a tutor for her once they were married—a promise he kept.

My in-laws' formal wedding portrait is a reflection of Shanghai in transition in 1929; it integrates both Chinese and Western elements. Ven-Long and his best man are wearing British-style morning coats and spats, while Yue-Fang and her bridesmaid are wearing white dresses (Chinese wedding dresses are traditionally red), but with high Chinese collars. A flower girl and ring boy stand on either side, both swathed in layers of fancy clothing; The ring boy made me smile; with his worried little face and thin bow legs sticking out of his short pants, he is a perfect picture of nervousness and suffering. Unfortunately, the names of all the attendants have been lost.

Grandmother Yin had bound feet and was illiterate, yet she was shrewd and strong-willed, ruling her large family with complete control. Chinese women were suppressed throughout history, playing second fiddle to their husbands, brothers, or older male relatives. Yet, like wild plants growing in the cracks of a stone wall, a few Chinese women did manage to gain power by using their wits and hard work. Think of the Empress Dowager Cixi, who rose from the rank of concubine to rule all of China.

Of course, women first had to survive childbirth; in some cases, they gained power by surviving their husbands because sons were supposed to mind their mothers. Grandmother Yin was one of these strong women, known to dominate not only her daughters-in-law but her own mother-in-law as well. When her husband took up opium in middle age, an atrocious habit quite common in China in the early 1900s, Grandmother Yin had the audacity to lock him in a room to "dry out." He came out later, shame-faced but unburdened by addiction.

So Yue-Fang married into this large Yin family. A daughter-in-law was supposed to serve her parents-in-law and help in running the household. This position entailed a lot of responsibility and relatively little fun. Shortly after the wedding, Ven-Long was promoted to head a new branch of his company. He took his bride and moved to Hankou (now incorporated into Wuhan), several hundred miles away from Shanghai. Her female relatives were all envious that Yue-Fang could taste the freedom of a "small household." Indeed, she spent a happy year with her adoring husband in Hankou.

When Yue-Fang delivered a healthy baby boy, Ted, the whole family was joyous. Ven-Long was away on a business trip at the time. In his eagerness to join his wife and new baby, he arranged to fly home. Aviation was then a new venture in China. He happened to be on the same plane with an important Chinese official whose elaborate departure was accompanied by an army band. After the plane took off, it circled back for a farewell salute to the dignitaries on the ground. The pilot's inexperience caused him to lose control, and the plane crashed. Ven-Long and a score of others were killed instantly.

The family didn't tell Yue-Fang of the accident until weeks later when her suspicion led her to burst out of her lying-in room. In her shock, she sat in front of the fire for hours every day, not eating and not feeding Ted, who was eventually cared for by a wet nurse.

The family was overwhelmed with grief, but Yue-Fang alone suffered the hellish life of a widow from that moment on. Her life, as decreed by the customs of upper-class Chinese society at that time, forbade all joy and color. She lived with her son Ted in the big Yin household—a crimeless prisoner with an endless sentence.

In old China, widows—particularly the younger ones—were considered unlucky, as if they had caused the deaths of their husbands through their faults, their bitter fate. I think all the mourning rituals were designed to torture the widows, thereafter called "the one yet to die." Yue-Fang wore mourning black for three years. For the first forty-nine days, she was required to call out Ven-Long's name at every meal time. The custom was to store his sealed coffin for a year before burial, and Yue-Fang had to visit his coffin every seven days.

A widow certainly felt miserable enough, but people expected her to be abject, to show no interest in life at all. Any sign of levity from a recent widow would be shocking, and Yue-Fang—at the tender age of twenty-four—lived a life, in her own words, "never short of food or money but a living hell nonetheless." Her only respite was to return with Ted to her father's home where she could relax a little and be herself.

Grandmother Yin didn't like that arrangement much but acquiesced because Grandfather Sun happened to be one of the few people she couldn't intimidate. At the end of the three years, Grandfather Sun had a dress made for Yue-Fang; it was gray with splashes of small pink flowers on it. That was the beginning of Yue-Fang shedding her blacks. Again Grandmother Yin couldn't object since her own father had given the dress to Yue-Fang.

There was never any question of Yue-Fang remarrying. The Chinese upper classes of that era disapproved of widows remarrying. Doing so would have brought shame to herself as well as Ted. Yue-Fang had hoped to go back to school or to work in an office, but those activities were not socially acceptable for a young widow, particularly a pretty one. Instead she developed her interests in cooking and sewing.

In the beginning, she bribed her nephews to allow her to sew for them since they were less clothes-conscious than her nieces. She also designed her own clothes. Whenever there was a big dinner party, the maids would gather nearby and wait to see what pretty, new outfit Third Mistress would wear. Yue-Fang also took cooking lessons and got to be good enough to cook for special occasions for the family.

Yue-Fang lived with the large Yin family for eighteen years in Shanghai. The Chinese Nationalist government came back to Shanghai in 1945 after Japan surrendered at the end of World War II, but soon lost the city to the Chinese Communist army. Chaos and turmoil were everywhere. The second Yin son and his family of six made plans to escape to Hong Kong. Grandmother Yin decided to go too and asked to be escorted by her favorite grandson, Ted. But Yue-Fang was not included in the plan. Ted was distraught, but Yue-Fang insisted that he go for safety's sake. She said, "Don't worry, I'll find a way to come—no matter what." Her mindset was clear: she would not be separated from her son for long, and she had full confidence in herself. After she was stymied many times, a relative finally helped her to get a tourist visa to Hong Kong in 1953. She and her son were reunited after three years apart.

After Grandmother Yin passed away, Yue-Fang finally got the chance to work as an accountant in a small firm in Hong Kong; she did that for ten years until she came to join Ted and me. Her abacus, which she used in her work all those years, still sits on my desk. I remember her right hand flying over it, gracefully pushing the wooden disks up and down along the thin steel rods as if she were playing a musical instrument, making pleasant sounds almost like that of a bamboo wind chime.

SEVEN

Carnage from the Sky

Young Chinese victim of Japanese bombing, 1937 © Everett Collection/Alamy

From 1938 to 1940, when I was six to eight years old, my family and I spent a third of our lives in air raid shelters, hiding from Japanese bombs. The shelters were tunnels dug into the rocky mountains, just tall enough to allow an average man to stand. The better ones had wooden planks to sit on, but in some you could only sit on the ground. When enemy airplanes came, people ran into the shelters carrying their children, a few valuables, and whatever food they had. In the damp darkness, they often huddled for ten or twelve hours—hungry, sleep-deprived, and anxious—and experienced the full spectrum of terror. To a child in wartime, chaos and bombing were constants. They dominated everything, with no relief and no escape.

In the early twentieth century, Japan emerged as a great power through its successful industrialization. Lacking in natural resources, Japan had long developed its "imperial expansion policy" of moving into other countries to gain territory and raw material.

At the same time, the Qing dynasty in China was overthrown, and the Republic of China was founded in 1911. However, the Republic's reforms were hampered by domestic chaos; warlords ruled different parts of the country for the next ten-some years and battled each other continuously. Thus, China—weak and disorganized, but possessing great resources—naturally became an attractive target for Japanese expansion.

Japan's approach to this goal was simplicity itself. It wanted to provoke China into war. Many Japanese citizens were then living in the northeast of China, and they instigated conflicts with Chinese citizens and then claimed mistreatment by the Chinese police. That provided a pretext for the nearby Japanese army to retaliate and occupy the territory.

China knew the weakness of its own military and, failing to get any help from the League of Nations, didn't dare to declare all-out war. Instead, it put up resistance in local skirmishes to slow the Japanese advance. In this fashion, the Japanese army, which was supposedly not at war with China, occupied part of Manchuria and later other coastal cities. Officially, the Sino-Japanese War started in 1937, but in reality, Japan began occupying parts of Chinese territory from as early as 1931. My parents experienced this firsthand as they were then living in Manchuria.

My parents' long exodus during the Japanese invasion of China took them from Shenyang, their first home in Manchuria, to Greenwood Fort, 2000 miles inland. One morning in 1931, my young parents, both new professors at Northeastern University, awoke to the sound of gunfire and soon found that the streets were full of Japanese soldiers.

The university officials realized that Japan meant to occupy Shenyang and immediately decided to move to Beijing. That became the pattern in China. Every time the Japanese military occupied a city or a region, there would be an exodus inland of Chinese key industries, professionals, civil servants, students, and those who did not want to live under Japanese occupation. They traveled by train, boat, bus, ox wagon, and often on foot.

My mother, pregnant with me, left Shenyang and traveled to Beijing alone by train as Father had to stay behind to organize the students' retreat. Even though war had not been declared, a Japanese fighter plane felt perfectly free to spray the civilians in the train with machine guns. To protect themselves from the bullets, Mother and the other passengers had to block the windows with luggage. Right then and there, she decided to name her unborn child Fei, which means "to fly" in Chinese. She intended for her first-born to grow up and serve in the yet-to-be-formed Chinese Air Force. (Sorry, Mami, I did not make it!)

I was born in Beijing in 1932. In 1934, Father was offered a position at the National Ministry of Education. Our family moved to the southern capital of Nanjing where Mother taught at the National Central University. Even with constant skirmishes against Japan in northern China, Nanjing was far enough inland to be relatively safe for a while, and I, doted on by my parents, had a peaceful existence for five years.

By 1937, Japan had occupied all of Manchuria and moved southward toward the doorstep of Beijing. China was forced to declare war. I believe that Japanese airplanes bombed the capital city of Nanjing the next day. People didn't know what was happening when the newly installed air raid alarm sounded. The bombs were raining down without any retaliation by China.

I was a clueless five-year-old, paralyzed with fear when my amah (nanny) grabbed me to hide under a tree. My one lasting impression of that dreadful day was our neighbor, a gentleman with impeccable manners, wearing a spotless long white gown, diving to the ground into a mud puddle. For some reason, while I was trembling under that tree, all I could think was that he would never get that gown clean again, not realizing that our lives—just as his dirtied gown—would never again be pristine.

The civilian casualties were heavy. The next day my parents bought boat tickets. My mother, Ah Yee, and I were to leave Nanjing immediately; Father had to stay behind to tie up loose ends. The last image I have of Nanjing was of a crowded and chaotic pier on that misty evening. My father hoisted me on his shoulders and patted my legs to reassure me that he would join us shortly.

It was great luck that my father got out of Nanjing just weeks before the infamous "Rape of Nanjing" by Japanese soldiers. Historians estimate that upwards of three hundred thousand Chinese people—mostly civilians—were tortured and brutally murdered. Countless women were raped and then slaughtered. The victims were ordered to line up, dig their own graves, and then shot as target practice by laughing Japanese soldiers. They were utterly defenseless, and their blood stained the Yangzi River red.

In a short time, Beijing, Shanghai, and Nanjing all fell to the Japanese, and the Chinese government retreated, step by step, to the wartime capital of Chongqing, in Sichuan Province. My mother, Ah Yee, and I stayed with friends in Wuhan for six months, then reunited with Father and arrived in Chongqing in 1938. Ah Yee found a teaching position in Shapingba, a suburb of Chongqing, and we all stayed in the housing provided by her school. Father commuted to his office in Chongqing weekly. Mother continued to teach at National Central University, which also had relocated to Shapingba.

The Japanese advanced toward Chongqing but were unable to force the Chinese army into a decisive battle. Their leaders realized that, by using bombers, they could shut down the Chinese government and break the will of its army to fight. Since China had few anti-aircraft guns and no fighter planes, our ability to retaliate was pathetic. So a group of Japanese bombers could fly four hundred sixty miles from occupied Wuhan to Chongqing, drop their bombs, and return safely after a three-hour round trip. Then another group of planes would leisurely repeat the same process.

The bombing went on from 1938 to 1942. The targets were usually residential areas, business zones, schools, hospitals, and other non-military sites. The Japanese intended to cow the Chinese government with these record-setting attacks. The bloodiest killing took place over two nights—May 3 and 4, 1939—when forty-four hundred civilians were killed. The longest continuous bombing lasted from May to September of 1940, all day and all night long for five long months.

The news media coined the phrase "fatigue bombing" for these attacks. Along with the Rape of Nanjing, the bombing of Chongqing was among the worst of Japan's atrocities against Chinese civilians. They had no limits in their cruelty to us. The air raids could come at any time: early morning, noon, or the middle of the night. Moonlit nights were of particular danger.

The warning signals were sirens and a system of red balls raised on a tall wooden pole. One red ball meant the enemy bombers were coming: "get ready to run"; two meant they were near: "there is no time left"; three meant they were right over Chongqing: "bombs are falling!"

A bomb was like a comet dropping straight from the sky. It didn't leave a trail of fire, but emitted a prolonged scream, piercing and otherworldly, as if coming from some mythical monster. To my child's mind, this horrible sound, "SHOOOOEEEEEEE," was coming straight at me. The monster landed with a loud "BANG!" followed by fire and pandemonium.

My family, like everyone else, made repeated trips between home and shelter, scrounging whatever food we could find on the outside. We were the lucky ones; countless others lost their homes or lives as half of the city turned into rubble. On many of these trips, my mother would try to shield me from seeing bodies on the roadside. I walked with eyes almost completely shut, clinging to Mother's arm, the only stable force in my upside-down, shattered world.

The Ministry of Education where my father worked was originally located in Chongqing. It moved its offices and personnel to a nearby rural village called Qingmuguan or "Greenwood Fort" in 1940, hoping that this farming community surrounded by tall mountains would be less likely to be bombed. Sure enough, the air raids did considerably lessen after we moved there. By that time, Japan had expanded its scope of invasion to other parts of Asia and the Pacific, and they could not keep up the constant pressure on China of previous years.

As soon as my family moved to our new home in Greenwood Fort, my father was hit by bomb shrapnel in a town thirty miles away. He was officiating at a university athletic meet when the air raid came. He and my cousin De, a student at the university, were busy talking and didn't enter the shelter soon enough. Father later said that he hadn't even felt the sting until he saw blood oozing from his shoe. He had been hit in the shoulder and leg.

I remember white-faced De running home to tell Mother the news. The adults huddled together to decide what to do and then hurried off to the hospital where Father had been taken. From then on, my mother, aunt, and cousin took turns staying with Father at the hospital where they had to feed him, bathe him, and carry him to and from the air shelter because the hospital was flooded with wounded people and extremely short-handed.

My family made sure one of them stayed in Greenwood Fort to take care of me. I was truly a terrified eight-year-old; the possibility of losing one or both of my parents constantly whirled in my mind. I tried as hard as I could not to be a bother to my family and fervently believed that if I were as good as I could be and prayed enough—to Buddha, Guanyin, or God—that Father would somehow be spared.

Father made progress very slowly as drugs were almost non-existent. After three weeks in the hospital, which was bombed many times during his stay, it was decided that he would be safer recuperating in our new home in Greenwood Fort. Shortly after Father came home, his leg became infected and swelled to enormous size. A doctor from the Ministry of Education came to open the wound so the pus could drain out. That was the time before sulfa drugs. I think that the doctor might have been short on anesthetics as well because, on his advice, Mother rushed off to the rice field so she wouldn't hear Father's screams.

Nobody paid attention to me, crouching under the bamboo trees outside the house. Entreating the gods to save my father, I buried my head between my knees and covered my ears with clenched fists, but I couldn't block out the terrible cries. Luckily Father did pull through this ordeal and survive. But, shortly after he was out of danger, Mother lost the baby she was carrying.

EIGHT

Refuge from War

Rural Sichuan © Paul Snook

Our house in Greenwood Fort had no electricity, no running water, and no sewer. Yet I remember it as an oasis during the stormy Sino-Japanese War, a haven from the continuous pounding of Japanese bombs and a nurturing place that helped a broken family to heal and be whole again.

Once the bombing stopped, our life at Greenwood Fort became surprisingly tranquil. Greenwood Fort was a sleepy farming community situated on a plain with miles and miles of rice fields. It was completely surrounded by tall mountains like a natural fort, thus its name.

At the start of the war, a highway had been constructed from east to west between two mountain passes. It was appropriately named the "New Road." All the serious commerce took place on the "Old Road," however—a narrower cobblestone road that ran through the only "town" in Greenwood Fort. Several hundred houses lined the street. Some of them were shops selling tofu, notions, bamboo sandals, etc. To shop for other daily necessities, we had to wait for the first and fifteenth of each month when farmers would come in from their villages carrying produce, meat, and a variety of other supplies.

Most of the farmers and new residents lived in villages—really just clusters of houses–scattered among the rice fields. Narrow dirt roads, no more than three feet wide and threading through the rice and vegetable fields, were the only connections between one village and another. One traveled on these roads mostly on the "No. 11 bus" (two legs). A more luxurious mode of transportation was to ride in a hammock slung between bamboo poles and carried by two coolies (manual laborers of the era).

Almost all of the people living in Greenwood Fort were poor. The farmers had little money to begin with. Those who came to Sichuan Province because of the war, nicknamed the "lower river folks" by the locals, had lost almost all of their belongings. The largest employer was the Ministry of Education, which paid meager salaries that, because of constant budgetary woes, were often delayed.

Despite the absence of money, we lived well. Thanks to the farmers, there was never a shortage of food. Also, labor was very cheap, so we had household help. Mother loved animals and learned to raise chickens, pigs, and goats with the help of our manservant, Yang. We had eggs from the chickens and milk from the goats every day. Of course the pigs were eventually sold to other people, as none of us could stomach the thought of eating animals we had fed daily.

The local watermelons were small but sweet, especially after being chilled in the well water for a few hours. When there was a particularly sweet one, my father liked to say, "Sugar is its grandson," an expression from his hometown in Caodian, meaning the watermelon was several times sweeter than sugar.

One summer day I was playing outside when Mother called for me to come in. I kept answering, "Coming, coming!" but was too engrossed in my game to stop. Father then stood by the door and said in a loud voice, "Boy, sugar is its grandson!" That got my attention, and I came running into the house where I found, not watermelon, but the adults laughing. Father smiled at Mother and said, "Didn't I tell you it would get her in the house in a hurry?"

When the Ministry of Education moved to Greenwood Fort, it commissioned local laborers to build houses for its employees. Ours was built in less than two weeks and sat on a low hill. The simple process consisted of erecting bamboo walls between weight-bearing wooden poles, plastering cement on the walls, and putting a straw roof on the top. The roofs leaked and the walls were more like room dividers, providing very little defense against the elements or thieves.

In our poverty-stricken region, petty thieves were common, and policemen, few. The thieves could cut a hole in these bamboo walls with great ease. Some liked to make a small hole first, to get a closer look at how the furniture was arranged—the better to plot routes of entry and escape. Sometimes the residents, upon waking, would find a small hole in the wall and be thankful that the thieves had not thought there was enough to bother stealing. The less intrepid thieves wouldn't risk entering the house but tried to lift clothing, shoes, or any small items through pried-open windows, using a long bamboo stick with a hook attached to the end.

Bamboo was the ubiquitous king of our household. We had bamboo beds, tables, chairs, sofas, cooking utensils, hats, sandals, umbrellas…. An eighty-year-old woman in the next village could weave bamboo baskets as large as a tree trunk or as small as a thumb. In the summer, a bamboo fan was a must, and a bamboo mat was a luxury.

The winters were damp and bitter. We occasionally enjoyed the luxury of a small charcoal fire. Most of the time, we slept under heavy bedding and wore padded cotton tops, pants, and shoes. The clothes were so thick that they hampered movement; they made me feel like a padded scarecrow with unbending arms sticking out on both sides.

On really freezing nights, I was given a bed warmer, a covered brass pot filled with boiling water that could be put under the bedding hours before bedtime. What a heavenly feeling to gingerly stretch my cold feet into that toasty bedding! Getting out of bed to go to school in the morning, however, was always a chilly affair and required many wake-up calls from Mother.

In the summer, everyone had to sleep under the protection of a mosquito net. The smaller ones had round tops, and the larger ones, square tops. Some of my imaginative friends caught fireflies and put them into their nets at night, so they could imagine that the stars were blinking at them as they fell asleep.

I remember a neighbor who probably had an obsessive-compulsive disorder and would unknowingly put on a show for the neighborhood kids every evening. He religiously fanned the four corners of his square net a hundred times each before closing the net. Oblivious to the children's giggles, he seriously believed that his ritual was a superior way to make sure no mosquitoes were inside the net.

I started second grade in elementary school at Greenwood Fort in 1940 and left before I finished eighth grade in junior high in 1946. The elementary school was some distance from my home, and the round trip required more than an hour. Picking up my best friend An, who lived nearby, every school morning, I had good company on these trips.

Our favorite pastime was reading "Chinese Westerns" on the road. The stories portrayed heroes, heroines, and villains—all of them experts in martial arts. Most importantly, the good guys possessed the traditional Chinese virtues of honor, loyalty, helping the downtrodden, and keeping a promise at all costs. In the less-than-perfect real world, these characters warmed our hearts.

The stories had endless intrigues and always lifted our spirits when the good guys invariably won. We probably read these books while walking on the narrow village roads because our parents didn't think too highly of them. Anyway, it made the trips to school exciting, particularly when we made a misstep now and then and fell into a rice paddy.

We had few playthings or toys, but endless fun. In summertime, when school was out, I would hurriedly finish my daily assignments. Once my diary entries, math problems, and calligraphy practice were done, I could play all day. The outdoor games included hopscotch, leapfrog, tag, and jump rope.

The fancier version of jumping rope was double Dutch. It was hard enough to enter the moving ropes from either side. To make it even more difficult, we jumped rope on the low hill in front of my house, so we had to jump and climb steps at the same time. I loved it and could jump rope for hours with my friends, oblivious to the sweat pouring down my body.

I well remember the refreshing sensation when I got a cold sponge bath afterward, as I uttered the long, delicious, "Ah…." Another favorite game was kicking *jianzi*, a small homemade shuttlecock with a flat bottom. I spent hours and hours practicing various maneuvers until I finally became proficient enough to land one on the side of my face or the top of my head at will.

One of our great indoor games was raising silkworms. My friends and I got their eggs from the farmers in late spring. They looked like little black dots on a piece of paper and had to be kept warm and in the dark. I placed mine inside a small cotton pouch tucked inside my clothing and checked them several times a day until I saw little worms emerging from the dots. Then I got busy picking mulberry leaves, washing them, drying them, and feeding them to the delicate, little silkworms, lovingly nicknamed "precious silk babies" by all. Wet mulberry leaves, which would make the worms sick, were absolutely taboo.

The silkworms grew rapidly; in early summer, their bodies became almost translucent, and their feeding slowed down. That was the time for them to make cocoons. Again, darkness and quiet were required; nobody was to disturb the precious silk babies. Slowly, they gave out silk from their mouths, and began forming cocoons on our straw supports of many colors—pink, green, lilac, and light blue. We then boiled the cocoons so they would keep a long time. The game ended with us excitedly trading our cocoons with our friends.

Once in junior high, I began to study more seriously. The high school was affiliated with the National Central University and noted for its high academic standards. To many students, the school was the only home they had, having retreated with the government while their families remained in Japanese-occupied territory. Tuition, room, and board were free for all students.

The meals of vegetables and rice were a constant subject of ridicule in the school newspaper but provided enough nutrition. I was one of the lucky "walkers" who lived and ate at home. The school classrooms were shabby, but I had some of the best teachers there. I believe that my seventh-grade math teacher, more than anyone else, inspired me to major in the sciences by making numbers and logical thinking fun.

Our house had a cement patio in front where the family gathered on hot summer nights—the sweetest time of day. After supper, our diligent servant Yang would wet the cement patio with water so it would cool off as the water evaporated. Then he would light mosquito repellent incense, which gave off a pungent but not unpleasant smell.

The adults sat on chairs in a circle and traded family stories while I stretched out on the bamboo lounge nearby, tired after playing with my friends half the day. Someone—my mother, aunt or cousin—would lazily scratch my mosquito bites and fan me now and then. I listened to the adults' murmuring voices absentmindedly and looked at the dark sky with twinkling stars, remembering the many tales Father had told me about the various constellations. Periodically, I would mumble a request to my "scratcher" to please change spots.

The long night lingered on pleasantly until I was lulled to sleep by a sense of deep contentment. It welled up in my small chest like a flower opening, blossoming, knowing that my family was all around me and we were safe from harm.

I left Greenwood Fort with my family in 1946 after World War II ended and Japan was defeated; I went back to visit China for the first time forty years later. I struggled over my itinerary for a long time and finally, with a sense of loss and regret, decided not to visit any of the eight places where I had lived for a total of seventeen years. So much had changed and so little could ever be recaptured.

My Greenwood Fort was an oasis amidst tall mountains that gave new life to a family almost destroyed by Japanese fatigue bombing. In my memory, it is forever the lush green fields shimmering under the morning sun; it is the small gurgling stream next to my school, tall grass and sweet smelling flowers carpeting its bank, with bees buzzing around; it is the moonlit nights on our patio with my family gathered to talk and laugh. Greenwood Fort is my youth when the summer was long and lazy, the air filled with the fragrance of new growth, and I played all day.

NINE

My Trip to the City

My family in Qingmuguan, Sichuan circa 1940. Front row from left: me, Father, Mother holding Hsiang. Back row: Cousin De, "Big Cousin," Ah Yee, Hoh Cousin

I could barely suppress singing out loud as I rushed to get dressed and eat breakfast on that gloomy wintry morning in 1943. I was going to the big city—Chongqing! To an eleven-year-old girl living in the Chinese countryside, the city promised an exciting modern world.

My parents and Ah Yee had gone to the city a week earlier for work, but I had to stay to finish my school examinations. My older cousin Yu suggested that he could put me on a bus to Chongqing. Mother was a little apprehensive, but I pleaded and begged. Finally, I convinced my parents that I could travel by myself. After all, I was eleven and all grown up!

My cousin walked with me to the bus depot, a wooden shack, and bought my ticket. Waving it in his hand, he said, "You're in luck. A freight truck will be here soon, and I got you a discount ticket to ride on it. It will go straight to Chongqing, and you'll be there sooner than we thought."

During the war with Japan, both vehicles and fuel were in short supply. All vehicles that could move were put to use for public transportation, and the fuel was a creative mix of gasoline, alcohol, and even charcoal. Unreliable schedules and frequent breakdowns were calmly accepted. Often, if a freight truck was not filled to capacity, places were sold to passengers who would sit on top of the cargo.

Soon afterward, a truck lumbered into the depot. What luck—it was only half full. My cousin swung me onto the back of the truck, and I quickly found a space on top of a wooden box. With my bag by my side, I happily settled in for the trip, very grateful that my mother had just finished sewing her old fur lining inside my winter coat.

The truck was soon filled with passengers. I urged my cousin to go back to work.

"Are you sure you're going to be all right?" he asked.

"Oh, yes, Big Cousin, I'll be all right. I promise not to move from this box."

My cousin politely requested that the people nearby look after "the little girl" and then left. I waited contentedly, entertained by visions of various adventures awaiting me in the city. Thirty minutes, one hour, then two hours went by, and nothing moved. I questioned fellow passengers around me. They sat on boxes and bundles, all thankful that they had paid discount prices for their places on this express freight truck. Nobody knew anything about the reason for our delay, but nobody was complaining, and nobody was leaving his or her seat.

Another hour crept by. The driver finally showed up and cranked the engine again and again. Thankfully, after what seemed an eternity, it caught with an explosive bang. The driver jumped in, and the truck began huffing and puffing up the mountain road. I breathed a long sigh as relief washed over me. Now I started to eat the candy my cousin had given me and looked around and enjoyed the scenery, feeling happy and grateful that I was on my way to a fun weekend.

The truck bumped and swayed along the rocky road, but I sat firmly on my box the best I could. In this happy mood, I hardly noticed the very slight discomfort from my bladder. A little later, it made itself known sneakily with more pressure. I shifted on my box and tried not to pay attention to it. It became worse and more insistent. I was worried at first, then gradually more and more alarmed. I tried looking at the tall mountains with their sharp peaks reaching skyward. I tried looking down at the gorge, so winding and rocky that its little creek burst into dancing falls now and then. No, no, looking at the dancing water was not a good idea. The stunning views didn't help, and my urge to go got stronger. I tried counting numbers backward. I tried crossing and uncrossing my legs. I tried pinching myself. Nothing helped. Why wasn't anybody else squirming? Was I the only one who had had a liquid breakfast? What was I to do if I couldn't hold it any longer?

Another half hour went by. By then only a single thought remained in my mind: how to end my misery without letting the whole world know. I tried gingerly lifting up the bottom of my coat, thinking that I might save the fur, but it was too late. I already felt the warm wetness in my underwear. My shame overwhelmed me. I could only hope that my clothes were heavy enough to soak up all the pee.

I don't remember much of the rest of the trip. I hunched over on the box, hugging my bag and folding my body to be as small and invisible as possible. As my clothes got colder, I glanced around; no one paid me the slightest attention. Mercifully, the truck pulled into the city depot five hours after I had first sat down on that box. With my wet underwear sticking to my legs, I struggled to get down from the truck, looking back stealthily to check if there was a telltale wet spot on the box. Thank goodness it was dry. The poor fur lining of my coat had already stiffened, after being so long in the cold.

I walked clumsily toward my parents' hotel with shuffling feet, trying to appear "normal" to the passersby. A moment later, I heard my name shouted excitedly. There stood my parents and Ah Yee right across the road; they had been worried about my late arrival and had been waiting for hours. At the sight of them, all my anxiety, frustration, and embarrassment gave way to one big loud sob, and I fell into my mother's arms.

As Mother helped me with a hot bath in front of the small charcoal fire in their room, I sobbed out all the embarrassing details of my torturous trip and my inconsolable regret over the ruined fur lining. Ah Yee said not to worry as she had a short coat that could be altered to fit me. My father kept saying, "Everything's okay. Everything's okay. We're not going to miss dinner or the movie."

At the restaurant, my parents ordered not one, but two of my favorite dishes. In the evening, I sat between my father and my mother, enthralled by an animated film unlike anything I'd ever seen before. Years later, I found out that the movie was the magical *Fantasia*, the reason my parents had invited me to the city in the first place. My memory of *Fantasia* is unforgettably entwined with that long, desperate ride that ended in the safe arms of my family.

TEN

A Foreign Student

Me in San Francisco, 1966

The Second World War ended and Japan surrendered to the allies and China in September 1945. I remember the firecrackers bursting out all around our house in the village of Greenwood Fort. People were shouting, dancing, laughing and crying. Our neighbor, who, in the last eight years, had lost a husband to illness and a son to Japanese bombs, came into our house wordlessly and put her head on my mother's shoulder, weeping as if her heart would never mend.

My family went back to Nanjing following the Ministry of Education. Everybody was busy settling down with jobs and lodgings. I entered the Jinling Girls' Middle School and had three years of undisturbed education, paying little attention to the conflicts between the Nationalists and the Communists. The next thing I knew, the Communist army was crossing the Yangzi River to attack Nanjing, and we had to move again. My father's cousin, who was in Taiwan, helped us settle there in 1949, in the lovely town of Hsinchu. My first impression was of wide streets and few people, the quiet occasionally interrupted by the "clack, clack" of the wooden flip flops the natives wore in this semi-tropical land.

In the fall of 1950, I entered Taiwan University after passing its demanding entrance examination. A year later I was hit by the fever of wanting to go abroad to study. I have to confess that it was not something I had long desired, nor planned, but many of my classmates were leaving Taiwan, particularly the better students. I realized that Taiwan was small and my future options limited, so I wanted to try for a larger world too.

My parents were surprisingly supportive in spite of the expected long separation. Mother later explained to me that the Korean War was at its height then, and Taiwan faced daily threats from the Communists; she and my father wanted their precious daughter out of harm's way and to get a good education, too. They realized, probably more so than I, that once gone, I would never again live at home; I would leave the warm, protective cushion that they had provided me all my life and face the world on my own.

Father wrote to his old classmate Harry Engleman, who helped me get a scholarship. For my expenses abroad, Mother sold a gold bracelet, which her favorite brother, my Fifth Uncle, had given to her when we left Mainland China, supposedly for emergency use only.

Before I left, both my parents described America to me as they remembered its land, people, and customs. Father told me stories about his college days with Uncle Harry. On the night before I left, my whole family traveled to Taibei and stayed overnight to see me off. Just before I boarded the airplane, Mother handed me a fat envelope containing many long letters she had written during the month before my departure—letters full of encouragement and support that I read over and over again on the airplane, amid unstoppable tears.

My family tried to keep up their cheerful faces for my sake. Years later, Mother told me that on the sad train ride home, my father finally broke down. "Baba locked himself in the men's room and cried for a long time. He had to wait until most of the passengers got off because he was afraid people would see his swollen face and red eyes."

I had an equally difficult time leaving home, and I was in tears most of the time during my first few months in America. But my mother's story of overcoming her homesickness, at an age a little younger than I was, sustained me.

On a sunny autumn day, I arrived at Western College for Women in Oxford, Ohio, a month after school started. The campus had magnificent old buildings and rolling green hills dotted by clusters of maple and ash trees just starting to show off their multicolored leaves; it was stunningly beautiful. Even in my sad state of mind, I knew that I would not forget this first sight of Western College.

Everything was novel and exciting. My introduction to my new environment was smoothed by kind and helpful schoolmates, teachers, and my serviceable English. A counselor helped me enroll in a few courses. They were not difficult except for Art Appreciation. My British-accented instructor would turn off the lights and show slides of Greek architecture and I, not understanding her English one bit nor knowing anything about architecture, let alone Greek architecture, was instantly lost among the Corinthian columns. I could only draw the outline of the slides furiously in the dark and borrow notes from classmates later to figure out what it was all about. The girls were willing to lend me their notes. My biggest problem was to remember the right girl and to find her again, as they all looked the same to me. Thankfully, in a few months, the details of each girl's face became more distinct, like a photo developing. Now I know why Westerners say all Chinese look alike.

Another difficulty was being put on "bell duty." Our dormitory had only one phone, which rang constantly on weekends. We few foreign students who didn't expect any weekend dates were the natural choice to answer the phone. Sitting in the phone cubbyhole, my nerves were frazzled. First of all, I couldn't understand who was being asked for. After much struggle, I would write the name down; then I had to go find the girl in one of the many rooms.

I had no trouble with eating Western food. In fact, I loved it. Mealtime was a relief from the homesickness and loneliness I felt all day long, particularly when I dug into the desserts.

Soon, I discovered something curious. Attending classes, the girls wore hair curlers and no makeup as if they had just gotten out of bed, even though they were required to look nice for dinner in the evening. One of them explained to me that it was because there were no boys present in the daytime. We all carried books in our arms to classes; each proud girl with a boyfriend would have a large, framed photograph of him on top of the books. Sometimes, one would "introduce" me to her boyfriend, "Fay, say hello to my Tom." Having been educated in a stricter Chinese school system, I soon realized that Western College, founded by alumnae of Mount Holyoke and now part of Miami University, was not a school devoted to scholarship. The unmistakable message was that to acquire a boyfriend and get married was the first order of importance. I didn't think much of that, even in the dark ages of the early 1950s. The idea that I should transfer to a better university started to take hold in my mind.

My worst memory of Western concerned the gym teacher, Miss James, who was in her mid-forties, stout, with very short hair and a pair of noticeably rough-looking hands. I had been a fair student-athlete all my life and loved gym class. From my first period in volleyball class, I was reprimanded much more than others. I just could not do anything right. If I missed the ball, I got yelled at, and if I saved the ball, I still got yelled at. I was so confused and overwhelmed that I often walked out of the class in tears. Some days Miss James would be unexpectedly jovial coming to class, slapping one girl on the shoulder and joking with another. But in another instant, she would turn to me and shoot me down. Finally, some of my classmates told me this was just Miss James' way. Each semester, she picked one or two favorite "targets" to be the recipients of her abuse. It helped a little bit knowing that, but I felt so helpless and unjustly singled out that I became afraid to attend my gym class at Western.

My first Christmas in 1951 was spent with the Englemans, my American family. To meet them, I did my hair up in two buns, one on each side of my head, and wore a *qipao* (Chinese high-collared dress.) It was the last time I was so attired; soon jeans replaced the *qipao*. On Christmas morning, I was flooded with presents. I couldn't imagine how they figured out that I needed an alarm clock, a winter coat, sweaters, and many other necessary items, only to find out that they had telephoned Western College and requested their help.

The Englemans made me feel at home instantly, and I became a lifelong member of the family. From that year on, I spent all my Christmas vacations with them. I slept in the room with their daughter Shirley, who guided me through everything I needed to know to be a co-ed. Every night I said good night to her in Chinese, and she replied in German, which she had learned from her grandmother. Uncle Harry's sister-in-law, Aunt Bertha, took me to Radio City in New York. Talk about an eye-popping experience for a foreign student! The Englemans gave each other joke presents as well as real ones. There was so much laughter in creating them and then watching the recipients open them on Christmas morning. Their kindness and caring made up for the absence of my own family.

With the help of Miss Bascom, Mother's last living professor at the University of Wisconsin, I transferred to Madison in 1952 and majored in chemistry. The campus, surrounded by scenic lakes, was big, beautiful, and vibrant. There were students from all over the U.S. and other countries—all eager to learn. The chemistry and mathematics classes, taught by marvelous lecturers, fascinated and energized me. I studied hard and also had fun. I got a job working in the cafeteria and went to dances at the International Students Club on weekends. My world opened up, and my life blossomed.

One early morning, without any planning, I sat down and wrote a long letter to Miss James. I detailed the unnecessary misery she dosed out to me that drove me crazy and almost ruined my otherwise favorable impression of America. I beseeched her not to treat her students like that anymore, particularly any foreign student before she found her bearings in this country. Of course, I didn't receive a reply, but I was proud of myself for having written that letter. Now, as I write about this incident, I think it was my transfer to Wisconsin that restored my sense of self-worth and enabled me to cry out against injustice.

I don't recall what induced me to go to my first Friday night dance at the International Students Club. I had never danced before in China. I watched with fascination the students learning and practicing couple dances. Their turning, whirling, and gliding on the floor, in time with the music, was like moving poetry to me. In no time at all, I started to learn to do the same, and I realized that I had found my sport and my hobby.

In my senior year, my science courses demanded a lot of time, and I developed a good routine; I would have physical chemistry lab all Friday afternoon, then dance all Friday night. Once I hurried back to my dorm just before the eleven o'clock curfew, I wrote my report on that day's experiments, sometimes finishing near dawn on Saturday. It was not a routine I would recommend to anybody, but it worked for me. I took advantage of my endorphin high after the dance and could write my detailed report in one sitting.

I met my dear longtime friend Delores Friedland at this time; she took me under her wing, taking me to the Student Union, introducing me to pizza on the Terrace, explaining dirty jokes, and telling me Wisconsin folklore. Science classes always took a lot of my time, and one year when a history examination came, I panicked because I had not prepared. Delores, a history major, said to me, "Okay, I'm going to summarize three important sections of early American history. Just study my summary and forget the rest." With Delores' help and an all-nighter, I got an undeserved A in the course.

To save money, I lived in a student co-op for a while. I remember my plan to eat on less than a dollar a day. I usually skipped breakfast, and lunch was a fried-egg sandwich from the corner shop across from the chemistry building. This way, I had more money for a better dinner. I usually "dined" at the Student Union cafeteria. For a penny a piece, the cafeteria offered delicious nut bread. I frequently indulged in two pieces and ate them last, biting off a small piece at a time, savoring the sweet, nutty flavor, almost like a dessert, while I gazed at the beautiful lake outside, with lights blinking near and far.

I graduated in 1954 with honors and got a scholarship to stay and attend graduate school in biochemistry. I talked to many professors about their various research interests and whether one of them might accept me. In this way, I ended up in Dr. Robert M. Bock's lab. He was one of the youngest professors on the faculty—bright, enthusiastic and full of research ideas. I learned everything from him, from elementary biochemistry concepts to asking questions, designing experiments, and studying the structure of the protein moiety of the ribosome, which became the subject of my thesis. I treasured my relationship with this kind and wise mentor, which lasted years after I left Wisconsin.

Most of the chemistry graduate students spent enormous amounts of time in the lab. The light blasted well into the night as many of us figured out it was easier to use the different machines at night than to fight with labmates during the daytime. A guy on the floor below Dr. Bock's lab would entertain us with his violin when he took a break near midnight, his instrument sounding like a chicken on its last breath. Occasionally, if there were enough of us left in the building near dawn, we would walk en masse to the bakery across the street to get bread fresh from the oven. So many times, I walked the short distance back to my room in the wee hours of the morning, feeling perfectly safe, and I was.

With its outstanding reputation, the biochemistry department at Wisconsin was a big family, friendly and nurturing for graduate students. We worked hard, and we had fun. If there was a home football game on Saturday afternoon, one could hear the battle cry, "Come on, come on! Let's go to the Field House. Don't let research interfere with football!" When one of us passed our preliminary oral exam for a Ph.D., the party would always be at the little bar nearby called "Hasty Tasty," more familiarly known as "Hate to Taste It."

The thirty-some Chinese students on campus had an association that sponsored dinner parties periodically. The ratio at that time between Chinese men and women was almost ten to one. If there was to be a party, the guys had to first phone the three girls, me included, to make sure the date was convenient for all of us. Otherwise, they would change the date so the ratio wouldn't get worse. Then the guys planned the party, bought the groceries, cooked the food, and chauffeured the girls to and from in one of their jalopies. I must say it was a good arrangement. The ratio changed slowly later on, and I heard the girls were no longer treated so royally.

With my busy course load, I did some dating but was not seriously involved with anyone. My limited free time was taken up with dancing, my never-waning interest. A fellow graduate student, Homer Epster, was a superb dancer and sometimes taught ballroom dancing. With no romantic feeling toward me, he nonetheless took me as his partner to many demonstrations. That pleased me, and I strived to do better and better.

In my first year in graduate school, I fell in "infatuation" with Gilbert Chang. He was an assistant professor of bacteriology, twelve or thirteen years my senior. I was fascinated by his story of some past romantic heartbreak and I was attracted by his worldly manners and handsome, melancholy face. We dated for many months, but I knew our relationship was hopeless as he would say to me about every other day, shaking his head slightly with a sad smile, "Oh, Fay, you're so young." I was terribly frustrated, but I could not age faster.

I was very unhappy in my predicament. Eventually my parents' images came to me and I thought that, being their daughter, I should not allow myself to linger in such a pathetic state. I decided to leave Madison for a while and wrote to various labs for jobs, eventually getting an assistantship at the Virus Lab at the University of

California, Berkeley. Dr. Bock kindly agreed to hold my place in his lab, as I would be learning techniques aligned with my own research.

I worked as a research assistant for a year in the lab of Dr. Howard Schachman, a renowned molecular virologist, where I thoroughly enjoyed learning a new research technique (ultracentrifugation) to study protein structure. Berkeley, where the liberal movement was already in the wind, was exciting and stimulating. My friend Delores had settled in Los Angeles by that time, and we did much traveling on the West Coast. We went into one or two pricey restaurants that she knew and shamelessly ordered one entrée to share. We got into the "hungry i" nightclub in San Francisco and paid a minimal price to hear the Gateway Singers and the Kingston Trio, who became famous folk singers later on.

In 1956, feeling more self-assured and refocused, I returned to Madison and resumed my studies in Dr. Bock's lab. A year later, I met Ted.

ELEVEN

Ted's Promise

Ted's graduation photo from Hong Kong University, 1953

Theodore Peng-Jung Yin was born on December 3, 1930, into a large, well-to-do family in Shanghai. He was often called "Teddy" by the Yins, as the Westernized Shanghainese people frequently used English names.

His father Ven-Long's early death cast a dark cloud over the family for many years. The one who suffered the most was his young mother; Ted fared much better—he was the apple of his grandmother's eye. In fact, he received special treatment because he didn't have a father. He grew up among scores of cousins, never lacking for playmates. Sometimes he returned to the Sun family home with his mother. There he was nicknamed the "King Cousin" because his maternal grandparents favored him as well.

The first hardship of Ted's childhood came when he was six years old; his mother decided to send him to a new boarding school—Shijie (World) Elementary School. It was fashionable for well-to-do Chinese families to send their sons to boarding school to toughen them up. Ted was terribly homesick, missing his mother and cousins, and did not like the school's routines at all. His mother and grandmother visited him every week at school. His sad goodbye to them always included the poignant request, "Please leave when I'm not looking." He was allowed to come home only on Saturdays, but Sunday came too quickly. I don't know how long he stayed in that school—presumably, the Sino-Japanese War put an end to it—but the unhappiness of that period made a lasting impression on Ted; he told me many times that he would never send his own children to boarding school.

Ted and his family didn't suffer unduly during the war when Shanghai was occupied by the Japanese because their house was located in the so-called "French Enclave." There, the jurisdiction and authority belonged not to the Chinese, but to the French. The Japanese made sure that their brutality didn't offend the foreign powers, so residents of the French, British, German, Portuguese, etc. enclaves were treated much better than other Chinese in the city. Ted's uncles were in trade, and one maternal uncle in particular became wealthy in the coal business, mixing loose charcoal with a flammable material, then shaping them into tennis ball-sized "coal balls," a new venture at the time.

Ted had always been a diligent student, and he finished his high school with honors. He had been thin his whole life, and he shot up to almost his full height of five feet ten in his late teens, achieving what he jokingly described as his "bamboo figure." In this period, he began to avoid walking with his mother out in public because she was beautiful and young looking, and his friends teased him terribly that she could be his girlfriend. It was much later that he was mature enough to be proud of a good-looking mother.

In 1950, Ted escaped to Hong Kong with his grandmother, Second Uncle, and his family of six; his mother had to wait for three years before she joined them. For the first time, the family lived in a crowded apartment rather than their spacious old house. Ted soon enrolled in Hong Kong University after passing its stringent entrance examination. The curriculum was completely taught in English; that formed a good foundation for Ted's mastery of the language.

Ted graduated from college with honors in chemistry in 1952 and began teaching at the Diocesan Boys School—a prestigious high school in Hong Kong. He was very popular with his students. One of them, Howard Un, said Ted was a superb teacher and credited him with sparking his interest and eventual career in chemistry. Howard told me that Ted was nicknamed "Shanghai Egg" by his students, a rare benign name among the many nasty ones dreamed up by the students.

Ted met his first girlfriend at that time, the daughter of a family friend who lived in the apartment downstairs. Theirs was a sweet, tentative first love. Unfortunately, her mother was a woman known to all for her acerbic tongue and cunning nature. His mother warned Ted that he should consider the consequences of such a union. Their love was thankfully interrupted when he left to study abroad.

Hong Kong was a suffocatingly small island, crowded with refugees from Mainland China. Ted wanted to leave and study abroad. This became his single-minded goal, but the arduous process took years. To obtain a passport from Hong Kong, Ted had to apply for it from the Chinese Nationalist government in Taiwan, which required him to spend six months in their army. So off he went to Taiwan to serve. He had his head shaved, practiced crawling in the mud and under barbwire, and ran for miles daily. Ted did it all with good spirits, knowing that six months was not long. He was lucky to have a kind-hearted sergeant who went easy on the "student soldiers." His worst bark was, "Run, you sissies! You should be ashamed of your skinny arms and legs!" On weekends, Ted and the other student soldiers went to the village to supplement their meager army rations. His friends introduced him to the Chinese bathhouse, which he grew to love.

For reasons not clear to me, getting a student visa to the U.S. was difficult for Ted; he shuttled between Taiwan and Hong Kong after he got out of the army, only to be turned down twice. In the meantime, he secured a research assistantship in the lab of Dr. John D. Ferry of the University of Wisconsin; Dr. Ferry was a well-known leader in polymer chemistry, specializing in rheology (the study of the flow of matter, which also became Ted's specialty). During this period Ted wrote many letters to Dr. Ferry about his visa problems and his on-again, off-again trip to the U.S. Dr. Ferry was apparently impressed by Ted's résumé and his persistence, and kindly agreed to hold the position for him for two years. He kept all of Ted's letters, written in his courtly British-trained voice, and presented them to the children and me when we visited him fifteen years after Ted died. All three of us were moved beyond speech.

A visa to Canada was easier to obtain than one to the U.S., so Ted applied for and received a research assistantship at the

University of Alberta in Edmonton, thinking that he could then transfer to Wisconsin later. When he showed his grandmother where he intended to study, she gasped, "But that's almost outside the map!"

Ted moved to Alberta in 1954. The language and curriculum were no problem for him. He found the cold unpleasant but bearable, but the food was his undoing. Eventually, he moved out of the dormitory and roomed with two Canadians who graciously consented to include rice in their simple dinners. After a few months, one of them, Vern Hosteadt, cheerfully remarked that he had eaten more rice than three generations of his family combined. Ted and Vern became good friends, and Ted somehow obtained a mah-jongg set and taught Vern and other friends to play the game. Vern was a sharp fellow; he liked to line up his tiles in groups of three and, in no time, figured out how to hold back the tiles that other players needed.

After he obtained a master's degree in physical chemistry, Ted finally transferred to the University of Wisconsin for his Ph.D. program in Dr. Ferry's lab. Dr. Ferry was an old-world gentleman, serious about his science, well mannered and kind. Ted had been trained in the British educational system and was also somewhat of an old-world gentleman. They got along very well.

On his initial days in the lab, Dr. Ferry made Ted follow him around. They would take measurements on a machine for two hours, then take a break, not by drinking coffee or eating donuts, but by doing other tasks in the lab. Ted learned discipline and critical thinking in the Ferry lab. His professor remained a friend during Ted's life and was later very kind to the children and me. Monona, in particular, developed a great fondness for Dr. Ferry and his wife, who treated her like a granddaughter. She visited them when her work took her to Milwaukee in the 1990s. The generous Ferrys took her out to dinner at "The Edgewater," a fancy restaurant that Ted and I as poor graduate students could only admire from afar. On their way there, Dr. Ferry made a special detour to Lake Monona so she could see the beauty of her namesake.

Madison, Wisconsin, forever brings back sweet memories, not just because it was the place where Ted and I met and fell in love, but also because we were both fortunate to have two amazing mentors there: Ted's Dr. Ferry and my Dr. Bock. In their respective labs, we not only learned scientific thinking and practice—which grounded our work for the rest of our professional lives—but were also nurtured with kindness and generosity. These two professors made our four years of graduate student life exciting and meaningful, with hard work but also fun. The children and I visited both of them several times and had wonderful reunions; we could never repay what they gave us.

We both received our degrees shortly after our son Duncan was born in 1960. Then Ted accepted a job at the DuPont Company so we happily packed up our newborn, our simple belongings, and moved to Wilmington, Delaware. Two years later, Monona was born, and Ted's mother joined us from Hong Kong to help when I returned to work, first at the University of Pennsylvania and, later, also at DuPont. For the next seven years, we lived in our first house, a normal happy family busy working and raising children. Ted did so well in his work that DuPont gave him six months' paid sabbatical to teach at the top university in Taiwan, and I got a leave from my department, too. His boss said that he would be promoted after he returned and transferred to a manufacturing site to gain broader experience as a future manager. All exciting news!

After we moved to Taiwan, my parents were overjoyed. They could now enjoy their grandchildren as never before and reconnect with their long-gone daughter and her family. Ted's mother was equally delighted as she went on a month-long trip to Hong Kong, her former home.

Ted taught a course on rheology, a new subject at Taiwan University, and was well liked by his students. In six months, he and I traveled all over the island and Hong Kong, renewing old friendships. We relished eating in all kinds of Chinese restaurants, after missing our native cuisine for so many years. Just when we were on top of the world, everything came crashing down. Ted died on January 22, 1970, in a freak accident at our temporary home. He was just thirty-nine years old.

TWELVE

Teacher of Teachers

Mother in 1971

My mother gave her last lecture at the age of ninety-two, marking the end of more than seventy years of teaching. On one of my many visits home to Taiwan, I accompanied her to this final lecture at Chinese Culture University. I sat way in the back and looked up at her standing at the lectern.

Mother's height had shrunk from five foot six to five foot four, but she invariably seemed taller because she always stood straight and never let her shoulders sag—the result of an iron will and life-long attention to physical fitness. Her hair was snowy white and still very full. She wore it in a style that made her look even taller. Her elegant coiffure and erect posture became her trademarks, and she cut a distinguished figure wherever she went.

Mother was known to be an outstanding lecturer. Her talks were always well prepared and delivered with eloquence. Every seat would be filled, even though she was also known to be a very demanding teacher. As schools in Taiwan became more liberal and informal, students frequently came to class late. Mother wouldn't stand for it. Each year at her first lecture, she would make it clear that she would do her best to teach and, in turn, she expected her students to work hard and be on time. If they couldn't do that, then they were wasting their time as well as hers. It was rumored that Mother's class was the only one at the university where students sat and waited for the professor.

On the day of Mother's last lecture, the classroom seemed even quieter than usual; nobody coughed or cleared their throat. Mother tired more easily then. Most of the time she spoke while sitting down, getting up only to write on the blackboard. Her hands showed the beginnings of a tremor, but her voice still projected well. She had carefully prepared the organization and content of this lecture, and it was excellent.

At the end, her voice quivered a little as she told her students that she would miss every one of them and miss teaching. She then wished them luck, success, and meaningful lives in an ever-changing world. They sat transfixed and, after a pause, broke out in thunderous applause. One after another slowly stood up and filed past the lectern to say goodbye to their old professor. Some of them held Mother's hand with both of their own, as if not wanting to let go. Everyone sensed that an era was ending.

Mother loved teaching and cared a great deal for her students. She firmly believed that teaching went far beyond book learning; she tried to instill in them a desire and practice to live a disciplined life with a balance of work, exercise, and personal joy. Many of her former students have written moving articles in magazines and newspapers about how Mother had a lasting influence on their lives.

My mother was lucky in that her open-minded father supported her desire to blaze new trails by going to Shanghai to study. She was hired for her first teaching job at Beijing Teachers' College at the tender age of eighteen after the college president chanced to see her student teaching. A year later, Mother's alma mater sponsored her to study in the U.S., where she majored in physical education with a minor in education.

In 1923, Mother came back to China with newly acquired knowledge and boundless enthusiasm to teach and make a difference. Over her long career, Mother held full professorships at three universities and was principal of an elementary and a high school. She enjoyed each position and felt richly rewarded, only leaving due to outside factors—her marriage to Father, the Sino-Japanese War, and later, the change of regimes in China.

By 1949, Mother had been teaching at the renowned National Central University of China for fifteen years. Then the Chinese Communists prevailed in the civil war, and my family moved to Taiwan with the Nationalist government.

As soon as Mother saw us settled in Taiwan, she flew back to Nanjing to finish her lectures for the university's graduating class. I well remember the day when large headlines in the newspaper announced the fall of Nanjing. My father, Ah Yee, and I were crazed with worry because Mother apparently didn't get out in time.

Two anxious days later, we got word that Mother had reached Shanghai and was on her way back to Taiwan. It turned out that she had caught one of the last flights out of Nanjing. By that time, with fighting nearby, Nanjing was in chaos and totally lawless. Mother told us that there was no way she could have reached the airport but for the devotion of four of her male students, who found a pedicab for her. Riding on bicycles and ignoring the possible risk to themselves, they surrounded the pedicab and escorted Mother all the way to the airport.

When the Qing dynasty lost the first Sino-Japanese War in 1894, it ceded Taiwan to Japan. The island was only returned to China after the Second World War. When my family moved there in 1949, Taiwan was still heavy with Japanese influences. Although local Taiwanese people spoke a dialect of Chinese, many of them spoke Japanese better than Mandarin—the official Chinese dialect from the Northeast. The government required much restructuring, particularly the education system, and teachers were urgently needed.

Mother was forty-eight years old in 1949 and had already spent thirty years teaching. With her experience, she was offered three work options by the Ministry of Education: teaching at the Teacher's College, being the principal of Taizhu Girls' High School—noted for its outstanding facilities—or being the principal of Hsinchu Elementary School.

Mother chose the third position for two reasons. First and fore-most, she firmly believed that elementary education is the founda-tion of all future education, having taught a course and done much research on the topic. Secondly, Hsinchu was close to Taibei where my father and aunt worked, and I attended college. After years of running and moving during the war, Mother wanted a home that we could all return to on weekends.

Hsinchu, known as the "City of the Wind" because of the con-tinuous sea breeze from offshore, had five elementary schools. At that time, Hsinchu Elementary School, or "Fuxiao" for short, was rated lowest of the five, infamous for having the smallest percentage of students to pass the high school entrance examination, as well as ranking last for years in interscholastic athletic meets. Its parents' association, headed by successful businessmen and professionals, acted much like a PTA in the U.S. but was more powerful. It often "made requests" to the school, and they were usually met.

Long Japanese rule had left many Japanese values intact; promi-nent among them was prejudice against women. The parents, already worried that their children were in the worst school, now had to accept a woman as principal. It was too much for them to take. They met and decided to go directly to the Ministry of Education to ask for Mother's appointment to be rescinded. Before the trip, the head of the parents' association met Mother by chance at a gathering, and was impressed enough to hold off temporarily to give Mother a chance. Nevertheless, many of the concerned parents transferred their children out of the school.

My mother rode her bicycle to work on her first day, two months before school was to start. I remember her describing her depressing first impression to us at dinner. Many classrooms were dilapidated, some had been turned into storage or even bedrooms for the custodians, and the school yard was knee high in grass.

Taiwan was years away from its economic boom and money was short everywhere. Mother convinced the thirty-six teachers that the school badly needed a cleanup, and the only way to get it would be to do it themselves. So, headed by Mother, all the teachers, custodians, and one nurse cleaned the classrooms, moved furniture, planted flowers, and cut the grass—not with a machine but a machete.

Mother told me that every evening when she rode her bike home, instead of feeling tired, she was filled with energy and hope. Shortly before school started, we moved into the principal's residence, a house right across the street from the school, which allowed Mother quick and easy access to Fuxiao. She made good use of it, spending long hours there, sometimes even after dinner.

However, the first letdown soon came. For the one hundred seats allocated to incoming new students, only seventy-five children applied—a sure sign of what the parents in Hsinchu thought of Fuxiao. There was no need for an entrance examination then; all seventy-five were enrolled. Mother was not discouraged; she thought smaller classes were preferable.

Mother launched many innovations at the school, and their beneficial effects were soon apparent after one or two semesters. Fuxiao still had many Japanese traditions when Mother took over. Physical punishment was the first to go. She emphasized balancing study with exercise and play. New additions included a small library, ping pong tables, and singing groups. (By the eighth year, there were twenty-six extracurricular activities.)

In the past, students had brought their lunches in aluminum boxes, which were eaten cold and in silence during the noon recess. Mother got a small grant from the American "China Aid Act" and used it to provide whole-wheat buns and nutritious soup, usually with tofu and seasonal vegetables, for every child at lunch. Large steam pots were bought to warm the lunch boxes. The children were allowed to talk and laugh during lunch, but they had to remain quiet and put their heads down on the table for twenty minutes of rest afterward.

Of all the changes Mother instituted at Fuxiao, the most amazing showed success only fifty days after school started, at the annual athletic meet of all elementary schools in Hsinchu. My mother believed that participation in physical fitness was most important for children and placed relatively little emphasis on winning. However, as always, she approached each project wholeheartedly and systematically. With the nurse and two enthusiastic young teachers—both graduates of the College of Physical Education—they started by giving students a physical examination, then tested their abilities and selected participants for each event. With a limited budget, the school hired local laborers to improve the athletic field, lengthen the runway, and dig a sandbox.

Student athletes practiced daily. The two coaches taught them the latest techniques in sports like high jump and broad jump, and runners practiced the baton exchange for relay races again and again until it was smooth. Each morning, after the whole student body did morning exercises on the school field, they stayed an extra twenty minutes to cheer on their schoolmates as they trained for various events. This routine energized the athletes as well as the other students who badly wanted their school to get out of the "basement." As the meet approached, eggs were added to the school lunch, and the parents' association donated red T-shirts with the school logo for the athletes.

Mother's other contribution was to compose a school song. Actually, she "borrowed" it from her alma mater—the University of Wisconsin—and wrote Chinese words to the tune of "On Wisconsin," which the school band practiced daily. Years later, some of the graduates of Fuxiao ended up studying in the U.S. and, when they chanced to hear "On Wisconsin" for the first time, immediately thought, "Oh, my God! They stole our school song!"

On the day of the meet, the whole school emptied out with palpable excitement. The "red kids" with their easy-to-spot T-shirts didn't disappoint; everyone gave his or her best, and fifty days of consistent practice finally paid off.

One highly dramatic moment came in the girls' four-by-one hundred-meters relay race. Fuxiao had already opened up a huge lead when disaster struck. The third leg runner tripped and fell! The young coach Pan, whose memoir recorded all the details, jumped up and down and yelled, "Get up! Get up and run!" The girl did just that and ran with all her might. Then the anchor leg runner, who was in last place when she got the baton, ran "like a motorcycle overtaking bicycles," and miraculously came in first by a hair. The whole crowd exploded with thunderous cheers. Some of the parents in the audience ran out immediately and spread the good news: the girls had won all seven events, and the boys, four. Fuxiao had easily won the overall championship!

In the late afternoon, the "red kids" marched in formation back to school with trophies in hand, followed by smiling coaches, teachers, principal, and the whole student body loudly singing Fuxiao's version of "On Wisconsin." Firecrackers popped on every street as they passed. Parents stood by clapping wildly with a mixture of disbelief and joy on their faces.

Fuxiao was no longer the weakling. The school's track and field teams went on to win consecutive championships for many years. Most importantly, this first win affirmed the students' belief in themselves and working together. They knew they had won because of the combined effort of the athletes and the entire staff and student body. This started a tradition of cooperation, hard work, and a deep love for the school. The parents began to view their woman principal differently from then on.

Another activity that raised the collective eyebrows of the parents' association was the installation of a communal shower in an empty classroom. Many of the children came from poor farming families with no plumbing; they came to school in bare feet and sometimes smelled. Mother wanted to establish good hygienic habits for the children and came up with a most unusual solution. My father had seen the setup in Finland and described it to her.

The "shower" was really just hot water pumped into horizontal metal tubes with holes in them. The children were taught to soap themselves quickly, scrub each other's backs, and then rinse themselves clean. With practice, the whole showering process took less than ten minutes. Those students without washing facilities at home were divided into groups and took turns washing themselves in the short hours after school.

The kids loved the showers! There was much joyful yelling and laughter in the shower room. Later on, even children with bathrooms at home asked to join the shower activities. I have seen photographs of the children in the act of furiously scrubbing themselves. They were all wearing white shorts, which I suppose the school provided as well.

One of the hurdles Mother had to overcome was a serious "request" from the parents' association to offer more tutoring. Getting their children into high school and college was the dream of every parent, and, since Fuxiao had failed miserably in the past, the parents wanted more tutoring. Long and grueling afterschool tutoring was the norm in all other schools at the time. Even though Mother was against it in principle, she could not flatly refuse the parents. She had to compromise.

First, together with the teachers, she put much thought into deciding how and what to tutor. Instead of memorization, lessons stressed understanding basic principles and logical analysis; students were encouraged to ask questions and even express their thoughts and feelings. This was unheard of at the time and became the hallmark of Fuxiao's teaching methods.

Parents were told that only sixth graders would be tutored, with the promise that teaching in the lower grades would stress math and reading fundamentals. Tutoring was to last no more than two hours with a fifteen-minute break in between. In the beginning, Mother stayed throughout the evening. She flicked the lights twice at eight o'clock sharp, as a signal for the students to pack their books and say goodbye.

Mother put her heart and soul into bettering Fuxiao, logging long hours at the school. I remember putting on a sour face when I came home on weekends from my university and found out that Mother was working. My father, however, was full of understanding and support. Instead of feeling neglected, Father was proud of what Mother was accomplishing. He often tried to mollify my hurt feelings by helping me with my English vocabulary in her place.

Mother was soon richly rewarded by her work. Once her innovations were established, the results were self-evident. The students were healthy, happy, lively, and mannerly (even in the absence of physical punishment). Within a short time, Fuxiao graduates led all Hsinchu elementary schools in the percentage of students admitted into high school, and later, college.

Of the thirty-six teachers Mother inherited, none was replaced, yet Fuxiao went from being the worst school to the best in one year—both in scholarship and athletic achievements.

The dominance of Fuxiao's sports teams was legendary. They so outpaced the other schools that, with the grudging consent of the students, they withdrew from interscholastic competition twice to give other schools a chance to win. Instead, in those two years, they held their own impressive athletic meets. Since my parents and aunt were well connected in the field of physical education, Mother invited many well-known coaches and sports stars to officiate their meets, and the students got a thrill competing in front of them.

Mother loved being principal of Fuxiao; her eight years and five months there were unquestionably the happiest of her long career. She once said, "Fuxiao is my finish line, my last job." Ironically her success was the undoing of her wish. The achievements of Fuxiao's educational system were so well known throughout Taiwan and even some parts of Southeast Asia that many schools sent teachers to Fuxiao to learn their methods.

The Ministry of Education eventually asked Mother to start a center to train elementary school teaching staff from all parts of Taiwan. Mother said, "No, no, I'll never leave Fuxiao." The parents' association, in a complete turnabout from their decision eight years before, sent representatives to the Ministry of Education to plead that their Principal Kao not be taken away. The Minister conferred with Mother many times and finally came to our house to persuade her with the argument that, "Benefiting a hundred schools is more important than benefiting one single school," to which Mother had no reasonable rebuttal. Eventually, she bowed to the pressure and reluctantly left Fuxiao to found the Elementary Teachers' In-Service

Training Center of Taiwan in 1956 in Banqiao, now a suburb of Taibei. She ended up staying for nearly eighteen years.

In founding the Elementary Teachers' In-Service Training Center, Mother started from scratch again—from designing the buildings and grounds to the curricula. She invited many of her colleagues to help, using Fuxiao as a blueprint. She set high goals for the center, envisioning that every trainee would return to his or her home school and teach, not by lectures alone, but by encouraging the children to think and question. They would teach children healthy living and good manners, extending beyond their school years.

On the practical side, trainees would learn innovative teaching methods and how to use new teaching aids such as audio-visuals, again a first in Taiwan in 1956. Equally important, the center would fortify the morale of schoolteachers (who were often overworked and underpaid) by sending visiting teams to rural schools and publishing a monthly alumni magazine. The motto of the center was "Good teachers foster a strong nation."

Every elementary school in Taiwan sent their best teachers and principals to be trained at Mother's center for one month. Their daily schedule was tightly packed with learning but also enlivened by extracurricular activities such as folk dancing, singing Chinese opera, gardening, flower arranging, and various sports.

Mother faced new participants every month, but she endeavored to know each one personally. It was her practice to line her desk with photos of incoming applicants and to glance at them occasionally to memorize their names and faces. New photos were displayed after she mastered the names of the previous set. Mother invariably made each person feel special when she addressed him or her by name.

With Mother's hard work and dedication to constant improvement, the Elementary Teachers' In-Service Training Center became another success story. In the fourteen years she was at the helm, more than sixteen thousand teachers learned innovative teaching methods at the Center. As described by the Chinese saying, "Teacher for one day, teacher forever," all those thousands of elementary school teachers who addressed Mother as Principal Kao became her lifelong students.

Mother retired a few years after Father, when she was seventy-three and he seventy-five, planning to enjoy a leisurely old age. Shortly afterward, Father was taking a short walk by himself at dusk when he was hit from behind by a motorcycle. He died two days later from his head injuries.

Mother was heartbroken; the grief and pain of losing Father was almost more than she could bear. Eventually she sought solace in teaching, her beloved vocation, by joining Chinese Culture University as professor and vice president a year later; that lasted another seventeen years.

During her long career, Mother received numerous awards, including an invitation from U.S. President Lyndon B. Johnson to present a talk at the World Education Conference in Asilomar, California, in 1967 and an honorary doctorate from Dankook University in Korea in 1983. She was well known in Taiwan as "Teacher of Teachers" and "Mother of Elementary Education."

I know the award Mother treasured most was the success of her students. With her wide connections in the educational field, she helped many of her students and colleagues rise in their careers, but she went much further than that. Her relationship with many of her students and colleagues was no less than that of a loving mother.

I well remember the happy occasion when two young teachers who met at Fuxiao got married. They had more than enough love for each other, but less than sufficient funds. Mother suggested they use the Fuxiao auditorium for their ceremony. In addition to helping with the decorations, Mother stepped up and officiated at the wedding. Afterward, our cook helped prepare a delicious buffet for the reception.

Instances like that were common, and many students and colleagues kept up with Mother for the rest of her life. After Mother's death, some Fuxiao alumni residing in the U.S. even contacted me when they gathered for reunions. Their love for Fuxiao and Principal Kao extended to me, simply because I am my mother's daughter.

I once went on a tour of Taiwan with my mother and Ah Yee; we were royally entertained by Mother's students everywhere. The last stop was a small scenic farming village on the southern tip of the island. As our train slowly pulled into the station, I thought I heard music from a radio. I was amazed and moved to learn that the principal of the town's only elementary school had come to welcome Mother at the station, complete with the school marching band and cheering students.

Mother died in 1997, just a month after her ninety-sixth birthday. More than five hundred former students, colleagues, and friends attended her memorial. Some of them got up at four a.m. to arrive in time for the service. In 2001, forty-five long years after Mother stepped down from Hsinchu Elementary School, the city of Hsinchu held a celebration for her one-hundredth birthday.

The mayor paid tribute to Principal Kao as the most beloved citizen in Hsinchu, not only for changing so many students' lives, but for putting Hsinchu on course to becoming a center of educational excellence. Many of Mother's students eulogized her by telling their own fond memories. At the buffet afterward, they rejoiced at tasting again the whole-wheat buns and tofu vegetable soup of their long-ago lunches at Hsinchu Elementary School.

THIRTEEN

Father of Chinese Athletics

Father circa 1970

My grandfather was known for his fiery temper and fearless spirit, expressed in the Chinese saying, "neither afraid of heaven nor earth." His son—my father—inherited a less explosive temper but was every bit as courageous.

During all of my growing up years, China was under Japanese attack. I was constantly terrified. The newspaper would report each defeat by saying, "the battleground has been rearranged." Reading news like that, some people would blame the Chinese army for not being able to hold its own; others got scared and would plan their next escape route.

Father, whom Mother described as hopelessly optimistic, would find something positive in the direst war situation and never blame the short-handed army. It was comforting and reassuring being around him, as if a little bit of his courage and optimism transferred to me. But I also knew that, if a retreat were necessary, Father would take care of it.

Even during those scary fourteen years, Father kept his boisterous humor, so our house was still a happy one. Scared, yes; pessimistic, no. Father had a laugh that came from deep in his belly as if he didn't have a care in the world. His favorite saying was, "My heart is as smooth as a freshly ironed handkerchief," meaning not a wrinkle worried him.

Every time we moved with the retreating government, Father was always the last one to "lock up," whether it was our house or his place of work. In the face of imminent danger, he was trusted to be capable and unafraid to do the last-minute work. Sometimes, though, he carried that fearlessness a little too far, which drove my mother crazy with worry.

For example, during the endless air raids, after he saw the rest of the family settled in the air shelter, Father had the habit of sneaking back outside to watch the few ground artillery shooting at Japanese airplanes. After being hit by shrapnel in one of those adventures, he almost died from an infection. That put a full stop to this habit.

Father oversaw physical education programs for all of China's youth for thirty-seven years. The job of improving the health and fitness of tens of millions of Chinese youth was no easy task; it involved changing people's fundamental concepts. Chinese people at that time had disdain or even contempt for physical education, which was thought of as "kids playing ball," an activity only suited for young people not smart enough to study. The concept that a good mind needed to reside in a healthy body was totally foreign. Father kept at it with determination, chipping away at the traditional Chinese view.

Father organized the Third National Athletic Meet in Wuhan in 1924. It was the first large-scale competition, and he was responsible for every one of the ensuing ones. The difficulties Father encountered, besides the usual ones of raising funds and organizing teams in a large country, would be considered ludicrous today.

Wuhan was under the control of a warlord Lu who had a heavy opium habit and usually took care of business around midnight when he was wide awake. To gain Lu's support and a donation, Father had to wait until the wee hours every night to do his convincing and negotiating.

After Lu pledged his help, the townspeople then rose in angry protests, first against building larger competition fields, which might change the good *feng shui* of the town, then against women participating in swim meets, which was considered too risqué. Father even received a letter threatening his life. Ever fearless, he convinced himself that what he was doing was important and went on planning as if nothing had changed. Thankfully, the competition went on and was a success.

During the war years, many schools had no athletic fields, and some didn't even offer a course in physical education. But Father encouraged or even insisted that everyone exercise, with participation rather than winning being the goal. During the hardship of the war years, young students coming together to compete in athletic events did foster a sense of solidarity and defiance against the brutality of the Japanese army.

For his continuing efforts to improve the physical well-being of Chinese youth, Father's alma mater, Springfield College, awarded him an honorary doctorate in 1961, and then in 1970, their Outstanding Alumnus Award. Mother and I accompanied him to Springfield, Massachusetts, the second time. Some of his old schoolmates welcomed me as if I were their long-lost daughter; they hugged me, laughed, and recounted the glorious stories of their youth.

A classmate's widow, Mrs. Helen Civiletto, learned that I had recently lost my husband, and was particularly kind and gracious to me. We developed a friendship of many years through phone calls, letters, and one memorable visit to her home, where she kept a roomful of old Springfield photos. Years later, she left me an unexpected bequest in her will; I was moved to tears.

Father was involved with the Chinese Olympic team as a leader or consultant for a total of nine Olympiads, from 1932 to 1972. He was instrumental in China's decision to participate in the Games for the first time. He convinced the political leaders that competing was worthwhile because it would raise people's awareness even though there was no hope for a medal. After they agreed, Father had to raise the funds to send the lone sprinter, Mr. Changchun Liu, and his coach on their month-long boat journey to Los Angeles.

China was then called the "sick man of Asia" and didn't win any medals for many years, but participating in the Olympics did open people's eyes to the inferiority of their young people's physical training and ability.

After the Communists took over Mainland China but before their government was widely recognized, Taiwan fought to continue representing China at the Olympics. Responsibility for the negotiations fell to Father, and they became more and more difficult.

The International Olympic Committee knew it couldn't favor Taiwan forever, to the exclusion of one billion Chinese on the mainland, but Taiwan's government and its people wanted to stay in the Games. So Father had to negotiate for Taiwan every four years against increasing resistance from the International Olympic Committee. The only silver lining was that he usually got to visit me on his way to a meeting abroad.

We sometimes talked about the struggle, both of us recognizing that Taiwan could not prevail for much longer. One evening in 1971, my neighbor knocked on my door with surprise all over his face to say there was a New York taxicab looking for my house. Imagine my shock to find my father in it! I had known he was going to Munich and would make a special detour to see the kids and me, but I had not expected him so early. After hugs and kisses, he told me that he was too tired to struggle with getting from the New York airport to Wilmington, Delaware.

I was so thankful that, as a seventy-two-year-old foreigner, he had figured out a direct (albeit expensive) way to come. We had a few unexpected wonderful days together; he played with his grandchildren, and I feasted on all the news from home. Father still sounded cheerful, but I couldn't fail to notice that the spring was fading from his step, and his laugh was not as hearty. We held onto each other a long time when I said goodbye at the airport. That was the last time I ever saw him before he died in 1975.

Because of the political tug-of-war, Mainland China didn't start competing in the Olympics until 1984. Beijing was the site of the 2008 Summer Olympic Games, and the host country put on a dazzling show. Now China was no longer a sports weakling; its athletes won one hundred medals, fifty-one of them gold. While watching the coverage with my daughter and granddaughter, I thought constantly of my father and his lifelong mission. Even though the civil war split the country in two, and Father was no longer alive to see the Chinese athletes, he would have been enormously proud of their astonishing success.

I only lived with my father for nineteen years before leaving home. Our later meetings were sporadic and brief, but some early memories stand out, becoming clearer and clearer as the years have gone by.

Father always doted on me. During all my growing up years, he didn't raise his voice to me more than two or three times. If I misbehaved and he gave me a slight reprimand, he would think of ways to make it up to me later, offering a kind of apology or excuse. My mother and Ah Yee made fun of him for being a soft disciplinarian.

During my infant and toddler years, the first thing Father said when he came in from work was always, "Where is the little one?" He did the same thing to one-year-old Monona and three-year-old Duncan when I took them to visit my parents in Taiwan in 1963. Again, the familiar question, "Where are the little ones?" If Monona was in the crib, she would stick up her bare foot, and Grandpa would make a big thing of kissing it.

My mother and Ah Yee took care of my daily needs and well-being and nursed me when I was sick. My father had a completely different role. He told me old Chinese stories, taught me poems, shared funny sayings, and showed me clever tricks. Our favorite was the "upside down mouth." I would lie on my back, and he would line up his face above mine, facing the opposite direction. When we both moved our mouths as if to speak, our upside down mouths looked ridiculous, and we invariably collapsed in helpless laughter no matter how many times we did it.

Dinner was our family time. Father loved to recount his whole day to us. If he went on too long, Ah Yee's attention would wander, and she would start to fidget. She would put some dish on Mother's plate and say, "Dip this chicken in that sauce. It adds a tangy taste." Father immediately feigned indignation, stopped his narration, and said sternly, "Okay, okay, because of your interruption, now I have to start from the beginning of the day again." Then a cry rose from the rest of us, "No, no, just continue from where you were. Please make it quick." Sometimes long after dinner ended, we continued arguing or laughing, depending on the subject.

I asked my daughter Monona what she remembered about her Ye Ye (grandfather), and she immediately replied, "Exuberance and energy." Father was always lean and fit. When he was in his mid-sixties, he impressed my new husband by getting down on the floor and doing fifty push-ups at my request, not even breathing hard. He taught Monona how to do a headstand and, to this day, she still remembers him instructing her, "Ahhhch (arch), ahhhch your back," with his Chinese accent.

My father and mother shared a love of physical activity. They took long vigorous walks and played ping pong and tennis whenever the facilities were available. Both of my parents were considered handsome in their youth. As they aged, Father and Mother made a striking old couple, with their straight backs, graying hair, and high energy.

Father's other outstanding characteristic was his openness and honesty. He told it like it was—sometimes a little too bluntly. He might get mad and yell at someone to his face, but would never say bad things behind his back. He took the optimistic road at every fork and somehow saw the good in everyone. He loved the game of Go and would drag home any good player he found for a match. The doorman down the street was his main opponent.

When Father traveled, he always brought home gifts for us—oh, the most inappropriately useless gifts! Like the fur-lined boots he brought from Finland for Mother to wear in semi-tropical Taiwan, or clothes for his grandchildren in the wrong sizes.

The back of Father's head had a steep ridge and, if a barber wasn't careful to taper his thick hair, he would expose about an inch of very thin hair, which looked almost white over the scalp. Father failed numerous times in foreign countries trying to tell barbers how to cut his hair. He finally took a large photo of the back of his head so the barber could see what he meant.

One year in Wilmington, needing a haircut, Father took out his photo to show me. I said I had the equipment and knew how to cut hair; I offered to do it for him. Doubt was definitely in his mind, but parental love won out. I convinced him I would do a good job now that I had seen the photo, which was worth a thousand words after all. Well, he had to walk around with a ring of white scalp for weeks. He told Mother later, "If she weren't my daughter, I would really have let her have it."

Father had lots of quirks and idiosyncrasies. He wouldn't eat crab, an expensive delicacy that we all loved. He said it was too much work to get to the meat. I suspect there was no gourmet food lover inside of Father. He wouldn't eat some Chinese dishes considered delicacies such as fish heads or chicken feet. I am his daughter; I won't touch these exotic foods either.

Once Father was the honored guest at a banquet in the Philippines, and the host politely put an entire roasted baby pig in front of him. Father not only didn't touch it, he turned his head so he didn't have to look at the pig. The poor host only caught on halfway through the dinner.

When I was thirteen and had just entered my first boarding school in Nanjing, homesickness plagued me like an unknown disease, and

I hated everything about my new school. On weekends I rushed home so my family's support and my favorite dishes could soothe my misery. My parents, about to take their daily long walks, asked me to join them one Sunday afternoon.

"No, I can't go. I have to study for the stupid English test."

Mother said, "Bring along your vocabulary list, and we'll help drill you."

The word I got stuck on was "insect." I thought and thought but couldn't recall its meaning until my father helped me out. He tried everything in pantomime: catching an imaginary butterfly, swatting a mosquito, chasing a grasshopper. I finally burst out laughing, yelling, "I've got it, I've got it."

Just then a long freight train appeared on the railroad tracks across the river. It moaned and roared, puffed and rattled, making so much noise that we couldn't hear each other talk. Finally, it slowly disappeared with a fading whistle and trailing black cloud—like a large, wounded dragon. We three stood there watching it go by. Since that moment long ago, I have loved the sight and sound of trains. This sweet memory is forever locked in my heart's treasure box.

FOURTEEN

My Mother-in-Law, Hup

My future mother-in-law at age 50 in Hong Kong, 1956

I lived with my mother-in-law for thirty-five years—twenty-five years longer than I lived with my husband, Ted, her adored son. After Ted died in 1970, our household was shrouded in darkness. Our little family was like four featherless birds blown out of our nest by a storm. We landed in a ditch of grief and fear, groping to go on without him.

"Hup" is short for Hao Po or grandmother in her Shanghainese dialect. Sadly, Hup had known tragedy before; she had lost her own husband when she was just twenty-four. Losing her only child, who had been her pride and joy—her reason for struggling on through long years of widowhood—was more than she could bear. Ted's death took away her dreams.

Hup tried to carry on the best she could, but there were times when she broke down in old-world grief, wailing and howling for an hour or more, calling her son's name. She seemed possessed by spirits, unable to hear or respond to us; tears dripped out of her tightly shut eyes, and her gaping mouth was a gash of despair. The few times the children and I witnessed her heartbreak were terrifying. We would hold her hands and cry our own tears, feeling completely powerless to console such unbearable anguish.

Hup came to Wilmington from Hong Kong in 1962 to live with Ted and me and the children. At that time, her relatives and friends were all happy for her. They said, "Third Mistress is finally reaping her reward now. Her reunion with her son's family has made all her sacrifices worth it. Isn't it wonderful that her old age will be such a happy one?"

Before her arrival, I was more than a little apprehensive about living with a mother-in-law whom I had yet to meet. I knew there was no alternative to this arrangement; Chinese widows of her generation didn't live by themselves if they had children. Ted had assured me that his mother was very easy to get along with, and this turned out to be an understatement. Hup was one of those rare people who always try to see things from the other person's perspective. Furthermore, if there was one thing Hup truly disliked, it was being a bother to others.

Hup was petite, standing less than five foot two and never weighing much more than a hundred pounds. Her face was a classic oval, with large, expressive eyes and flawless skin. She was beautiful and, being from Shanghai, had a sense of fashion and what looked good on her. Hup was always simply but immaculately dressed, even if there was nobody to see her all day long. If she was still wearing her morning gown when I came home from work, I would become immediately alarmed that she was ill.

Hup dyed her hair until the end of her life and always styled it in a bouffant. Until her fifties, she had looked like a movie star with a glamorous up-do. Later, when her hair thinned, she would point to it and say, "I look like a beggar now." Even when she was ill with cancer in her late eighties, she always managed to look at least ten years younger. Hup's beauty was impressive in its unchanging quality, as was the strong discipline that made it so.

I started working at the University of Pennsylvania shortly after Hup's arrival in 1963. Our son Duncan was two years old and daughter Monona, six months. A babysitter cared for the children, but Hup gradually took over the cooking. She loved it, and no effort was too great for her culinary art. Sometimes she would serve a favorite dish for each member of the family. She delighted in giving large parties that involved cooking for days on end. All that cutting, chopping, marinating, steaming, and frying, she performed happily. She felt richly rewarded when guests asked for second or third helpings.

After Ted died, Hup and I became comrades in our effort to go on living as a family, taking care of the children. Luckily it turned out to be a remarkable partnership that gave us both security and autonomy—a rare combination for a Chinese mother-in-law and daughter-in-law. A friend jokingly said that we were a couple—I was the husband, and Hup was my wife. It was true to some degree. I worked, chauffeured the children, and took care of yard work and repairs. Hup cooked, did the laundry, shopped for groceries, and

sometimes sewed clothes for Monona and me. She even reuphol-
stered the sofa once with the help of a friend. I didn't know of any
wife who worked harder than Hup; taking care of the three of us
became her life.

In the early days after Ted's death, when Hup's pain was as raw
as mine, she was more considerate and thoughtful toward me than
I had any reason to expect. Because of her own tragic experience as
a widow, she knew how to help me. Hup knew when I needed to
be alone; at other times she would subtly suggest that my friends
include me in their gatherings.

A year later, when I developed an interest in folk dancing, Hup
was totally supportive. Many nights she would sit with the children,
eating pizza, watching their favorite TV show while I went dancing.
I had enough Chinese upbringing in me to feel self-conscious about
going dancing as a widow, but Hup's wholehearted support made it
so much easier for me.

After the children went away to college, Hup and I settled into a
quieter and simpler routine. Now most of the dishes on the dinner
table were my favorites. Since my office was only a seven-minute
drive from home, I got into the habit of phoning Hup just before I
left work. Dinner would be steaming on the table when I stepped
through the back door.

I usually asked Hup about her day, which she often spent alone,
but she would tell me about the phone calls from relatives and friends,
or letters from Shanghai. On long winter nights, we would linger over
dinner, and Hup would tell me about her life.

After our life regained relative normalcy after some years, Hup once said to me, "If you ever want to remarry, don't let me stand in your way. I can find a place to live nearby, and you can still look after me." I laughingly replied, "Hup, if I ever find someone who can give me a better life than you, you'll be the first to know."

It was Hup's special brand of selfless consideration for others that endeared her to her nephews, nieces, and their spouses among both the Yin and Sun families. She didn't just cook goodies for them. At various stages of their lives, Hup served as babysitter, confidante, assistant midwife, and marriage counselor for a score of them. Even the in-laws trusted Hup because she was always fair in settling any marital dispute.

When relatives came to visit, Hup would spend days shopping and cooking, even preparing spring rolls from scratch. She would say to me, "Don't tell them how long I spent cooking. They would feel bad—and they would think I'm so slow." She was not slow; she just did everything with meticulous perfection.

Hup kept her insatiable desire to learn all her life; it helped her make friends as well. When she was in her eighties, literacy teacher Linda Johnson came into her life. Hup studied diligently with Linda; she made piles of little cards for new vocabulary words and sometimes would study her textbooks well into the night. For many years, on Thursday afternoons, Hup would have her books, notes, and dictionaries on the kitchen table and a pot of tea brewing, waiting for Linda's arrival. It was indeed a proud day for Hup when Linda invited her to give a short speech at a party for Literacy America, to talk about the trials and joys she experienced learning English. I watched with pride as well.

Hup developed a deep interest in Christianity late in life. She studied the Bible at home every week with a neighbor, Bruce Laird. In addition to the notes and dictionary, she also had an atlas so she could follow the various locations mentioned in the Bible. She did her homework faithfully and read a passage of the Bible every night before going to bed, even though she never went to church. Bruce understood, knowing that Hup's sincere belief was no less than any churchgoer's.

Characteristically, she became good friends with Bruce and his wife Ruth, and many lunches and theater trips followed. Hup, like a lot of Chinese speakers, had a hard time differentiating the sounds of "L" and "R," so they became "Bluce and Luce." They didn't mind and even laughingly referred to themselves as Bluce and Luce.

When a colleague of mine at DuPont wanted to learn Chinese for business purposes, I got him together with Hup. Charles Ford came for Tuesday evening lessons with Hup for many years. Hup was very serious about her teaching and ordered numerous textbooks from Taiwan. Hup refused any offer of payment from Charles for the lessons. However, she was delighted when he installed deadbolt locks on our doors as a way of showing thanks.

Hup was generous to a fault with others, but for herself she practiced old-fashioned Chinese frugality. She rarely threw anything away. In fact, she was a full-fledged pack rat. Every article of clothing and every utensil and gadget was treasured. When she was sure she would no longer need it, she would clean, wrap, and label the item, then store it in the attic. I was just the opposite; I loved to clean out my clutter and throw it away. I frequently packed boxes of clothing and left them for the Goodwill truck to pick up, only to laugh helplessly when I came home from work and saw Hup wearing my discarded garments.

Hup made many friends of various ages and backgrounds, many of whom were not Chinese. Her English might have been less than fluent, but her sincerity and generosity were obvious to all. Our neighbor Janice Keenan, who lived across the street and owned a Chihuahua, couldn't wait to open Hup's Christmas gift each year. It was always a different little outfit for her dog—one year a tuxedo, another year, a cape with Christmas trimmings. Years later, after she moved away to Easton, Maryland, and gave up driving, Janice cared enough to hire a car to drive her all the way back to Wilmington to attend Hup's memorial service.

Hup elevated housework to an art form. She had five different ways to get various stains out of a dress, get the kitchen floor shining, or to make meat tender. Quite frequently, friends would call up and ask Hup for tips on cooking, sewing, or cleaning. I particularly enjoyed her foolproof method of catching an annoying fly in the house. She would wait until it was dark outside, then turn off all the lights but leave the TV on. Sooner or later, the fly would seek out the light and land on the TV. Then Hup, waiting patiently on the sofa, would sneak up on the fly with a piece of wet tissue and catch it without fail.

As a perfectionist, Hup did most things well. However, driving got the better of her; she was never comfortable behind the wheel. Shortly after she came to this country, when she was in her late fifties, she tried to learn driving from Ted. That endeavor came to an abrupt halt by mutual agreement when it threatened to put a dent in their smooth mother-son relationship. Later, Hup learned from a professional teacher and eventually got her license. She was so small that her head barely peeked above the steering wheel. In the early days after she got her license, our neighbors were taken aback to see an apparently driverless car cruising down the street. The only driving Hup did was to the grocery store, but that was an enormous help to me.

Once when the children were in their early teens, and I was away at a professional meeting, their gerbil food ran out. They begged Hup to drive them to the pet store. Hup said "no" because her driving wasn't good enough. A torrent of protests and pleas came forth:

"Oh, Hup, if our gerbils don't eat, they'll die. You wouldn't let that happen, would you?"

"Your driving is good; all the neighbors said so. You'll have no problem driving us to the pet store."

"You can drive through Oak Lane Manor. There's no traffic there, and you can drive very slowly."

Hup stood her ground; she said she had never driven with passengers in her car and that it would make her nervous. The children had a solution for that too.

"We'll lie down on the back-seat floor; you won't even see us or hear us."

Hup's resistance eventually broke down. The children squeezed themselves on the floor of the backseat and didn't utter a single sound while Hup swallowed her fear and drove to and from the store. The children's pets were saved by Hup's valor.

Hup's self-discipline was legendary. When she decided to quit smoking in the early 1970s, she did it quietly with no announcement, resolution or fanfare. We found out only when we stopped seeing her with cigarettes. Hup quit smoking cold turkey and never resumed the habit. Her promises were guarantees. Her nephew used to say, "If Auntie says she'll go out and do something for you, rest assured that she'll do it even if it's raining knives outside."

Hup's life experiences led to a heightened sense of fair play and justice. She was forever sticking up for the underdog. When a young Chinese woman, barely able to speak English, was badly mistreated by her husband, it was Hup who persuaded Ted to get a lawyer for her. I belonged to a women's group. I once tried to explain to Hup what a liberated woman is and asked her if she'd like to hear some of the lectures. She laughed, "Ai ya ya, I'm afraid I'm too old to be liberated." However, in the best sense, Hup was a liberated woman. Whatever her life's situation, she always acted according to her own morals; she was fearless in the face of life's adversity, unbowed and dignified.

Hup loved sweets, and her favorite lunch was often a large piece of pie or cake. She also loved perfume, trinkets, Chinese opera, pretty clothes, and all gadgets—the newer, the better. I teased her that she was a "New Age grandma" because she knew a lot more about the new gadgets advertised on TV than I did, and she was willing to try anything that might be useful at home. Even in her musical tastes, Hup was modern. She started to listen to Dolly Parton and the Judds before I was even aware of the existence of country music.

After Duncan and Monona went away to college, Hup would prepare mountains of food for their homecomings. I remember one year before Thanksgiving, their arrival schedules were such that I had to pick up Duncan first at the airport, then turn around immediately to meet Monona at the train station.

Hup had pots simmering on the stove and pans slow-roasting in the oven. I asked her if she wanted to come along for the ride. She looked around and said with surprise, "Can you believe I'm already ahead of schedule? Let me change, and I'll go with you." It was early evening, and the setting sun painted the western sky a pearly pink. Hup was looking at the new construction on I-95 and asking questions. All of a sudden she said in English, with wonder, almost like a little girl, "One family, four people, all move same time. One in airplane, one in train, two in car. Wonderful, huh?"

Hup found a small lump in her breast in the summer of 1980. Two weeks later she had a complete mastectomy. She went through many kinds of physical therapy for almost a year to regain the use of her arm, never complaining or showing any self-pity. Then she enjoyed a remission lasting fourteen years.

Every three months I took her to see her oncologist, Dr. Stephen Grubbs, who routinely pronounced her in good health after his examination. He never failed to offer a cheerful goodbye by saying, "Whatever you're doing, keep it up, Mrs. Yin. Boy, oh boy, I hope I look as good as you do when I'm in my eighties." Hup would giggle a little, enormously pleased. Afterward, we would go out to eat at her favorite restaurant, and she would insist on treating me.

In 1995, my own mother in Taiwan began having health problems. I made many trips to Taiwan from that time on, heartsick at watching my mother's slow decline. I felt helpless and torn by my inability to simultaneously care for my two dear mothers who were separated by an ocean.

In 1996, Hup turned ninety, and we gave her a big party at the Hotel DuPont—Wilmington's finest. She looked radiant in a Chinese gown that she had sewn for herself out of a jewel-toned paisley. She was surrounded by her dear relatives and friends. Both Duncan and Monona paid tribute to her and spoke about the huge influence Hup had had on their lives. It was a splendid evening, and Hup was extremely happy and content.

Shortly afterward, I left for Taiwan and hired a caregiver to stay with Hup. Three weeks later, I came back to Wilmington, emotionally and physically exhausted from the strain and fifteen-hour flight. Hup had waited up for me, as she always did. Later, the caregiver pulled me aside and said softly, "Mrs. Yin has had these red pimples on her chest for many days now, and she wouldn't let me call you in Taiwan." My heart sank, knowing that her cancer had returned. The next day, we rushed to Dr. Grubbs. Hup started one kind of chemo-therapy after another, but none worked.

Hup was extremely calm. With total trust, she left all her medical care and decisions to me. I had the feeling that she went through the treatments more for my sake than for her own. She lost her appetite, had no energy and stayed in bed a lot. Nevertheless, insofar as she could, she followed her daily routine. She still insisted on locking the back door, which had been her responsibility for years. After she had difficulty walking, she would lean on the washer and a cabinet to get to the back door. Every morning, I would give her a mug of Ensure and take her blood pressure. It wasn't medically necessary, but it was a way for me to make a connection with her in the morning, a chance for some pleasant exchange.

Like many Chinese people her age, Hup was reluctant to talk about the inevitable end. She had been sending a little money to her sister's family in Shanghai for years. One day she said to me, "I told them that I won't send money anymore." I understood that she meant after she was gone. I replied that, since the sum was small, I could continue to help. Hup said, "No, no, I told them, like cutting nails (a Chinese expression meaning an irreversible no)."

She reached out and put her small hand, covered with age spots and purple veins, over mine, and said to me gently, "You've done enough. I know it's been terribly hard for you." I couldn't answer because my throat was so constricted. I understood that she was tidying up her affairs and showing her appreciation for me. She knew that there was no need to thank me because I cared for her out of love, and she accepted it as such.

When Dr. Grubbs told me that he would arrange hospice care for Hup, I knew the end was near. Hup would get up from bed to use the bathroom and for meals, eating less than a bird. The rest of the time she lay in bed, very peacefully listening to Chinese opera. A hospice chaplain, Reverend Dale Lance, came to visit Hup many times. They got along well. He would sit by her bedside and talk with her; Hup enjoyed that.

After Monona came home to help, Dale visited again and said that Hup wanted us to pray with them, which we did, holding hands. I don't remember one word of the prayer, but I remember Hup's smile at the end when she turned to Dale and said simply, "They really love me." For someone so self-effacing, it was an extraordinary statement of pride and contentment. Monona and I both cried, sensing how close the end must be.

Shortly after that, Duncan came home. Originally, the kids had arranged to take turns caregiving while I took a much-needed break. As my departure date neared, however, I decided not to leave because Hup was so weak. In this way, without causing any extra bother, Hup managed to bring us all together for a final goodbye. The night that Duncan came home, the three of us joined Hup at her bedside. She gathered up her strength to hold us close and say a long prayer. We sensed how important the moment was to her, but none of us realized it was our last night together.

With typical toughness, Hup got up on her own and walked into the bathroom. She washed her face and brushed her teeth as she always did, then carefully rinsed out her silver cup, which she had used for more than fifty years, and put it away in its usual place in the medicine cabinet. To the end, Hup never let her standards slip. The next morning, she lapsed into a coma.

For three days until she passed away, we sat with Hup, soothed her, held her hands and talked to her. We cried and laughed as we traded Hup stories. It was as if the world had temporarily stopped spinning. Inside our house, all was quiet and peaceful. Duncan, Monona and I spent seventy-two hours doing nothing else but caring for Hup, comforting each other and reaffirming our family bonds. That was Hup's last gift to us.

Many relatives, friends, and neighbors came from near and far to attend Hup's memorial service; we paid respect to a tiny woman who had the heart of a giant. Hup radiated simple goodness, integrity, and courage, which touched everyone around her. We were the lucky ones whom she loved above all.

FIFTEEN

Mother's Last Years

Reminders of my mother: her glasses, painting,
calligraphy, teaching notes, and letters to me.

On rare mornings, upon first waking, still drowsy with sleep, I've had the distinct sensation that my mother was in my apartment with me. I have no explanation for this; I hadn't dreamed of her the night before nor thought about her in recent days. Perhaps I woke up more refreshed than usual, feeling warm and secure—as I had when I was small, and Mother was nearby and taking care of things. Re-experiencing this momentary bliss makes me bury my head in the pillow and linger in bed a while longer, forgetting that my mother has been gone for almost twenty years.

I left my home in Taiwan in 1951 to study in the U.S. and eventually decided to stay. During that long separation—until my mother died at age ninety-six in 1997—she and I were rarely together except for short visits. However, I never felt distant from my mother or my family. She and I wrote to each other each week without fail for more than forty years, until her hands shook too badly and we replaced the letters with telephone calls. We exchanged more than two thousand letters!

My father and aunt were no less loving than Mother, but they were sporadic letter writers because they knew Mother was so diligent. She had a habit of carrying an aerogram, the self-folding kind, in her bag at all times. Whenever she had a moment, either waiting for someone or sitting in a boring meeting, she would write to me.

My heart never failed to leap when I caught sight of the beautiful and strong handwriting on the familiar blue envelopes in the mailbox. In my life in the U.S., first as a student, then as a wife and mother, and still later as a widow and single mother, how I relied on the support and love that poured out of those letters.

Every Saturday morning, the first thing I did was to write home; it was a meditative and restorative practice. In the sad years after my husband Ted's death, my burdens and worries lightened because some of them shifted onto my mother's shoulders. Telling her stories about her grandchildren made me so much more appreciative of what I had. The love of my family, in the U.S. and Taiwan, kept me afloat on stormy seas during those years.

Mother kept me up-to-date on what was going on with our family and friends. Her letters brought me right back home to Taiwan. I could hear the family dinner conversations and smell the aroma of my favorite ginger chicken. She always shared her inner thoughts and feelings—her joys and disappointments in work and life—and she listened to mine. Life had given her a lot, but she had to overcome severe hardship as well. We traversed many mountaintops and valleys side by side. In one letter she wrote, "It is six a.m. and everyone is still asleep. How interesting it is that we are the only two of our family awake at this hour, separated by thousands of miles of land and sea, yet so close."

In the letter that I treasure most, she wrote, "Of the tens of thousands of daughters on earth, you are the best."

Mother's last letter to me was never mailed; I discovered it while sitting with her when she was already very ill. I had learned to massage her face, which seemed to help her fall asleep. I usually stayed in the room for a while longer in case she woke up. I chanced to look in a drawer and found the familiar blue aerogram with only three words on it, "Dearest Bei Bei" (Mother's pet name for me) in her shaky handwriting with no date, probably written quite some time ago. I looked at her emaciated body on the bed and realized that it was Mother's last letter to me. Did she know that she would no longer be able to write to her daughter ever again? What had she wanted to tell me when she sensed that life was slowly fading away?

After my father had died in 1975, Mother was inconsolable for well over a year; she had lost her lifelong love, ablest counselor, and best friend. She didn't cry or talk about Father a lot, but she sometimes gave the impression that she was only half the person she had been before. She shunned all the activities she used to share with Father. There were no more long walks in the countryside, no more watching of familiar television programs.

Finally, Mother was persuaded to come out of retirement at age seventy-five to become the vice president of Chinese Culture University and teach a few classes as well. She thought being busy in her beloved work might take away some of the unbearable pain, which it did. She joined a group of friends that sang Chinese opera and took up painting at the same time, so she didn't have to be home as much. I remember Mother apologizing to me shortly after my father died: "I didn't do enough for you when your Ted died; I didn't know."

I took early retirement from my job at DuPont in 1991 to spend more time with my mother and aunt. We had about four good years and two awful ones. In the beginning, our meetings were filled with joy. My mother and Ah Yee invariably met me at the airport, waving their handkerchiefs wildly among the waiting crowd. Mother didn't like to see me off but always delighted in welcoming me home. In the initial torrent of conversation about their lives and mine, they always offered me wonderful food. Sometimes it would be long past their dinnertime, but Mother and Ah Yee never failed to sit with me, enjoying the sight of me devouring everything, with satisfied smiles on their faces.

I slept in the double-sized bedroom with them, which we called the "girls' dorm." Mother usually rose at dawn, as was her habit, and would often put her hand gently on me to check if I was cold, sometimes adding a light blanket. Frequently, I was awake but feigned sleep, knowing that Mother enjoyed doing it. I also luxuriated in reverting to my child self, who was so well cared for. We had days filled with scheduled activities and days of doing nothing except enjoying one another's company.

At ninety, Mother still walked with a straight back and kept happily busy by teaching a few hours a week and taking lessons in

Chinese painting and opera. Mother had grown up in a family that appreciated Chinese opera. My grandfather was a real connoisseur, and all my uncles could sing arias of one opera or another. Mother had a deep voice, so she sang the part of *lao sheng* or "old man"—the Chinese equivalent of bass. She went to her tutor once a week and painstakingly learned each aria the old-fashioned way. There were no written scores; her tutor would sing a verse, then Mother would repeat it. They were accompanied by her tutor's *er-hu*, a two-stringed musical instrument. She often listened to tapes of famous opera singers and then tried to emulate their delivery, practicing over and over again. She only sang the parts of honorable men: the fair father, the just official, the loyal friend, or the brave soldier. Mother said only when she sang as these men could she really get into the roles. Villains would not do.

On the days Mother taught, my aunt and I would accompany her to the university. Mother was known to be an excellent lecturer, and her class was almost always fully attended. I sometimes sat in the back of the classroom, enjoying her lecture and feeling so proud of her. Mother was invariably in great spirits afterward; my aunt and I teased her that she was on a "lecture high." Mother would always say, "Come on, I'm hungry; let me treat you to our favorite restaurant."

Sometimes we would play three-handed mah-jongg for fun. Ah Yee was an expert player, Mother a remedial second, and I—a hopeless novice. It would take me a long time to sort out my tiles. Every time my turn came up, I had difficulty figuring out which tile to play. Needless to say, I was dreadfully slow and made mistakes right and left. Mother and Ah Yee laughed a lot at my expense, and Ah Yee would jokingly say: "Ai ya ya, playing with Bei Bei is like riding in a broken cart pulled by an old bullock. For all the time I'm sitting here waiting, I could have finished embroidering a pair of slippers."

Mother used to be a good walker. In their sixties, my parents developed the habit of taking long walks. Mother said the walks not only benefited them physically but also allowed them to focus on one another exclusively, to truly talk and listen about family matters and their professional lives as well. They usually walked along the rice field near their home in Banqiao. On good days, they would reach the next town, have a bowl of noodles in a small café, and return the way they had come. A young student at the nearby high school had watched them often enough and interrupted their walk one day to present a poem in which he praised the "white-haired old couple, walking tirelessly day after day...."

After my father died, Mother couldn't bear to walk the same road without him and eventually stopped taking long walks altogether. Ah Yee did not like walking but loved playing mah-jongg, which she gave up so Mother wouldn't be left alone for long hours. Whenever I was home, we would often take a taxi to Taibei, Ah Yee to visit her mah-jongg friends and Mother and I to visit the botanical garden. We would walk with our arms linked together like a pair of young students. We talked and talked, moving freely from one topic to another. Sometimes she reminisced about old times; I particularly liked to hear about my childhood and my family's home life since I went away:

"The combination of pneumonia and whooping cough almost killed you when you were three. First, you had pneumonia. I was standing next to Dr. Zhang when he listened to your lungs. Do you still remember him? Kind of fat and jolly? He stamped his foot and said, 'Oh, no, now she has whooping cough—just what she doesn't need.' My heart just sank. The house turned into a small hospital and Ah Yee, your amah and I watched you around the clock. It took you almost two months to recover, and you had to learn to walk again."

I mentioned the time I flunked my fifth-grade math test and came home with a tear-stained face: "You not only didn't scold me, you gave me some sweets to make me stop crying."

Mother reminisced, "Yes, I wanted to encourage you to try again. Math is like that. Once you lose self-confidence in the subject, it loses you quickly. I know because it happened to me in grade school. I never got the hang of math after that."

"Thank you, Mami. Because of your encouragement, I did try again and got to like math eventually; it formed the foundation of my scientific career."

At other times, Mother talked about the pain of our separation. Each of us regretted that I had only lived with my family for nineteen years. Leaving home for the U.S. in 1951 was the hardest thing I had ever done in my young life. I wondered out loud how I had gotten the gumption to do it. Mother said they could not bear to let me go either, but more importantly, they wanted me out of harm's way in case Taiwan was attacked.

I relayed many stories of my life in the U.S., all of which I had surely reported in my weekly letters, but I never tired of repeating them and adding details, and Mother never tired of listening.

My mother and father visited me in the U.S. several times. Because of the expense of international travel, they only managed to come when they attended meetings abroad. The few times we got together left us with endless memories. Mother liked to recall when she came to visit Ted and me shortly after we got married and were living on campus at the University of Wisconsin. Ted and I were newly converted, enthusiastic fans of football and followed the fortunes of our football team religiously. One weekend, Wisconsin played an away game and won at the last minute. Mother reminisced:

> I listened to the radio with you and yelled just as loudly. Then you got the bright idea that we had time to drive out to the stadium to welcome back the team. We got there just in time to see the football players' bus pull in. You and Ted ran with the other fans toward the bus. I wanted to be a good sport and hurried along with you; actually, you two half-carried and half-dragged me. We sang and cheered around the bus, as if winning the game was the most important thing in the world. It wasn't until we got back to the car that I realized I had lost the heel of one of my shoes!

In 1964, when Duncan was four and Monona was almost two, I took them to Taiwan and spent three glorious months with my family. When we left to go back to our lives in the States, my parents had to endure grieving again. They returned from the airport, saw the toys left behind in the kids' room, and cried on each other's shoulders, missing their grandchildren and not knowing when we would be together again.

Then in 1969, our whole family including Hup spent six months in Taiwan, a joyous reunion that ended in tragedy. We still could not bear to talk about that time.

Thankfully, thirteen years later, Monona returned to Taiwan and made happier memories. She spent a year studying Chinese after her sophomore year at Yale. She lived with my mother and Ah Yee, and they so enjoyed each other's company. Mother said: "Monona and I were buddies. We usually spent the whole day together, going into the city in the morning—she to her school, and I to mine. Sometimes, if we had time, we would stop for breakfast at the soy milk and fried crullers stand. Then we met again in the afternoon, and I often took her to my evening social events so I got to introduce my wonderful granddaughter from Yelu Daxue (Yale) to my friends."

I shared that Monona's year with her was also one of the most satisfying events for me. I rejoiced at the thought that the two people I loved most in the world were getting to know each other in depth: "Monona often said that being with you changed her sense of herself and her place in the world. In her letter to her brother, she aptly wrote, 'Nai Nai is the combination of Maria Montessori and Mr. Chips.'"

Monona had grown up as a nobody from a small family in the U.S., but in Taiwan, she was the granddaughter of a revered teacher who was widely known and recognized. She also met all of our relatives. I said, "Now she feels connected to all those aunts, uncles and cousins on both sides of our family."

Mother also talked about her disappointments:

"You know, I've been frugal all my life, but we never seemed to have much savings. Now I regret that I didn't travel more with your father. After we stayed in Berlin and London for the Olympics, we wanted to go back to Europe. I loved the small, colorful cottages with window boxes full of blooms. Now it's too late; we have enough savings, but your father is gone."

Then, of course, we talked about my brother Hsiang, my junior by nine years and a mere child when I left home. A rather thoughtless and selfish person with a failed marriage and many affairs, he had brought much disappointment and distress to the family. My parents and Ah Yee doted on him and gave him all the love they gave to me. Mother had breastfed him for more than a year, and I still remembered Mother and Ah Yee staying up nights when he was sick. He was an adorable baby who turned into a troublesome teenager, a poor student who failed to get further than high school, and an indifferent husband and father who depended on Mother to support his children. He let her down repeatedly, and yet she never gave up on him. Mother said, "You know I believe in educating with love. While I had much success with my students, I failed miserably in bringing up Hsiang."

I countered, "No, no, Mami, on the contrary, I believe you succeeded. He has a job as a mechanic and has stayed in his second marriage. The children from his two marriages have given you much joy. Without the love you, Baba and Ah Yee gave him, he might have fared much worse." During my many visits home, I had limited contact with Hsiang. He was rarely home, even when Mother was very ill later on.

My mother's health was good for so long that I fooled myself into thinking that she would go on like that. When she first started deteriorating, it was hardly noticeable. Then a few years after she retired from teaching at ninety-two, her hands began shaking so badly that she couldn't write any more. On many late afternoons, we two sat together in her study. The setting sun, filtered through the patch of bamboo outside, made intricate shadows on the wall. We read and reread well- wishers' letters to Mother from Taiwan and other parts of the world; I marveled at the outpouring of love and concern. I knew a few of the writers, and Mother often said a few words about the ones I didn't know—how they met, how long she had taught them, etc. Then she dictated, and I wrote the replies. Mother was always upbeat; she said she was eating and sleeping well and thankful for what she could still do. Occasionally, I would write a Chinese character wrong, either reversing the two halves or getting the strokes wrong. That made Mother laugh. She would correct it and then say, "Well, you're not doing too badly for someone who has been away for so long."

I often walked with Mother, thinking that any exercise was better than none. When the walks in the botanical garden became too much for her, we walked in the yard. When she had difficulty lifting her legs, we retreated to the hallway. Mother would put her arms over my shoulder and walk forward while I supported her, walking backward. Mother said we were like two drunken tango dancers, and we laughed, trying not to think of her worsening condition and all its terrible implications.

A while later she started losing weight even though she was still eating and sleeping all right. Gerontology was still in its infancy in Taiwan, and all the tests available came back as normal. Gradually, her walking became less steady and her sleep more fitful. Her doctor was one of her former star students and the president of a well-known university hospital. He tried his best but could never find why she was gradually losing her strength and weight.

I increased my visits to Taiwan, but my mother and aunt were never at the airport to welcome me again. The one-hour car trip had become too much for Mother. Instead, she and Ah Yee would anxiously wait for me at home. Mother usually had her hair done and was well dressed for my return. However, each time there was less of her, and she looked more disheveled. Even her welcoming smile drooped. It shocked me to see Mother looking dejected; it just had never been her way. Finally, Mother stayed in her reclining chair most of the time, with no appetite and no energy. She didn't change out of her pajamas anymore for my return, and she could no longer get up to put her arms around me.

The last painful year went by too slowly. My flight usually landed in Taiwan in the evening. As soon as I could make out the lights on the island, my stomach began to twist into a knot, knowing that I would find Mother worse than the last time. The most frustrating part was that the physicians could find nothing to help. We bought a walker, wheelchair, bed pan, and diapers. We were lucky to have a kind young woman from the Philippines, Josephine, to help care for her. Later, we recruited another nurse so there would be someone present around the clock. Mother, who had been the quintessential caregiver in our family, now needed help with every daily task. Her mind was lucid to the end; she had no illusions about what was happening to her body.

When Monona visited her Nai Nai in 1995, the last bittersweet get-together for our three generations, Mother was still able to play word games with us, but her once sparkling intelligence was now imprisoned by her physical disabilities.

I remember the sad day when Mother haltingly spoke about her death in the near future, "Take care of your aunt and forgive your brother." It's a Chinese custom to send death notices to organizations one is involved with. Instead of writing replies to her friends' letters, I sat in the same study, eyeing the same shadows on the wall, and listened as Mother listed the organizations from her wheelchair. There were so many.

Mother stayed in bed most of the time yet didn't get any rest. The days and nights merged, laden with sadness bordering on despair. I often sat with her, sometimes holding her hand and sometimes massaging her face to help her fall asleep. Unfortunately, it worked only for a short while. In desperation, I held Mother in my arms and chanted a short prayer that I had learned in yoga class, "Oh my lord, oh my lord, be with me, be with me. Oh my lord, oh my lord, set me free, set me free." Mother liked it and chanted with me in her weak voice. Neither of us had any religious background, and yet the chanting offered us some comfort. I imagined Mother being set free from the shackles of her dying body.

Leaving Mother again was the hardest task. I often had to return to Wilmington because Hup was not in good health either. Usually Mother would watch me pack my suitcase, not saying a word no matter how much she wanted me to stay. On the day I was to leave, I often invited Mother's favorite student, whom I called "Sister Chen," to come and be with her while I slipped away. It was a cowardly act on my part; I didn't have the heart to say goodbye, not knowing how Mother would be when I returned the next time. Yet a selfish part of me wanted to leave, to get a break from the hopelessness of watching Mother's decline.

My mother died in October 1997, barely a month after my mother-in-law. My two mothers who had loved me without reservation, each in her own wonderful way, left a void in my heart that couldn't be filled. For a long time, my memory, like a car with a defective steering wheel, couldn't concentrate on the past joy and laughter but kept veering toward the pain. I couldn't think of them without seeing their emaciated bodies and gaunt faces.

Physically and emotionally exhausted after Hup's death and memorial service, I didn't make it to Mother's bedside before she died. Her two nurses told me that her last words were, "I love you. I love you." Could Mother have also been thinking of her absent daughter? My feelings of regret and guilt made the pain worse.

My ever-loving aunt, who was eighty-eight and frail herself, had carried the brunt of Mother's caregiving. Ah Yee died four years later, the curtain falling on the last of my elders. Since my aunt's death, I haven't returned to Taiwan, a place of so much loss and heartbreak for me.

Years later, after I moved out of my house into this apartment, life seemed to stabilize a little and the pain that eclipsed everything else diminished. Some memories of the happier times came back. Perhaps it's because I wanted my mother to see my beautiful new place that sometimes I sense her presence here. Knowing that she would have forgiven my absence at the end, I have been gradually able to forgive myself. I wish she could see my many orchids thriving in front of my large window overlooking a small forest and stream—exactly the kind she loved to grow.

You left me, sweet, two legacies—
  A legacy of love
A Heavenly Father would content,
  Had He the offer of;

You left me boundaries of pain
  Capacious as the sea,
Between eternity and time,
  Your consciousness and me.

  — *Emily Dickinson*

SIXTEEN

Letter to Ted

Ted with me and the children, Wilmington 1964

Yesterday I walked into the spare bedroom and happened to glance at our old family photo in which you, with your thin arms, circle me and the children, ages four and two. My heart skipped a beat! I was surprised by the pain, so familiar from long ago, yet muted by the many years that have gone by. Your tiny smile was trying to break through, but you were gazing forward seriously through your black-rimmed glasses. A life with so many blessings and so much promise, cut short by a freak accident.

It has been so long. Sometimes I'm even afraid that one day I'll forget what you looked like.

How many times during the forty-seven years since you left me have I yearned to talk to you? I wanted you badly at times: to talk about our children, our struggles, your mother—whom you left in my care and who devoted her life to us—our short, happy time together and a thousand small incidents....

Twelve years from our first date—that was all we had together. Remember your first phone call to me in 1957? You said, "You don't know me. My name is Ted Yin, and I'd like to take you out. My cousin Henry Yin gave me your name and thought we might enjoy each other's company." I was flabbergasted. In the 1950s, young Chinese men didn't call girls whom they didn't know and just bluntly introduce themselves. I think I put you off twice. Eventually, we went out and had a great time together. We talked a long time, amazed and pleased that we shared many of the same values and expectations. I remember that, for some reason, I said that I knew nothing about cars but I did love the looks of the Thunderbird. You jumped up and practically shouted, "Oh, I can't believe that we see eye-to-eye even on something like that!"

You were in chemistry and I in biochemistry; our school buildings were only a block away from each other. You were tall, slender and dapper; wearing your glasses and favorite tweed jacket, you looked almost professorial. Soon the people in my lab started to tease me, "Hey, Fay, I just saw your boyfriend in the library." Between studies and lab work, we saw a lot of each other. I had the atrocious habit of working late into the night in the lab; you gradually shifted to my schedule, too. Your professor, Dr. Ferry, was used to seeing you in the lab early, and couldn't figure out what made you change.

You were smart, considerate and kind. Neither of us could cook, but you lived with a group of young Chinese men and had to cook for them once a week, so you at least had more practice. When I had some American friends over for dinner, you volunteered to help me buy groceries and cook the few dishes you knew. As you were not included in the party, you worked all afternoon then quietly said goodbye and left. When I had out-of-town friends to visit, you drove your jalopy to pick them up from the airport. Unbeknownst to me, you carefully did a dry run first, to make sure you knew the way. You had no macho hang-ups, no vain ego, and I appreciated that. Many years after we married, I brought you to my first lab party at DuPont, and my boss said to me afterward, "You married well." He said it as if I had married someone with wealth or status. He must have sensed, behind your agreeable manner, your sharp mind and quiet strength.

We got married in Berkeley Heights, New Jersey—the hometown of my father's best college friend, Uncle Harry. He and his wife, Aunt Erla, were my surrogate parents in the U.S. My non-letter-writing father wrote him a note that simply said, "Please give Fay away for me." He knew he didn't need to say more—the Engleman family took care of our whole wedding! Their daughter Shirley was my maid-of-honor, Aunt Bertha was the organist, son-in-law George and son Bob were the ushers, and Aunt Erla prepared a delicious buffet for the reception. Your uncle's whole family came down from New York, and my cousin made it in time to be your best man. My parents and your mother couldn't come because of the exorbitant cost of airfare, but their happiness was obvious. We felt very loved during our small, simple wedding. Our budget honeymoon—one week in Washington, D.C.—was as amazing to two graduate students as any lavish trip we could have imagined.

Our first home was in Madison, Wisconsin. Huntington Court, wasn't it? We invited a few good friends over for Chinese porridge to celebrate our wedding. With our inexperience, we used three times the amount of rice needed; later, every storage container in the apartment was called to duty, and we ate leftovers for a week.

Most of our early married life was taken up with studying. Luckily, we both got our degrees just after Duncan was born in 1960. He was not a planned baby, coming when we were both so busy. But we couldn't have loved him more if we had been waiting for him for years. He was a good eater and a good sleeper. We had no experience at all with childrearing, but reading Dr. Spock and bumbling around, we managed to care for him while studying for our doctoral exams. Remember our panic when he cried? And if he didn't cry, we panicked that he might not be breathing!

Soon, you got a job offer from the DuPont Company, so we moved to Wilmington. Then Monona was born in 1962. Lovely: a boy for you and a girl for me. Hup came from Hong Kong to complete the family. I started to work at the University of Pennsylvania and commuted daily until I got a job at DuPont, too.

Blessed with a live-in babysitter and two incomes, we made time in our busy lives to enjoy ourselves. On weekends, there were always movies, concerts and—to humor me—lessons in ballroom dancing. We also traveled a lot, thanks to Hup. Our first time in New England, I couldn't get enough of lobster and crabs and devoured them daily. You went along with this diet for about three days but then said pitifully, "If I don't get some rice in me, this Chinese guy is not going to make it." Luckily, we both loved the French cuisine in Québec.

Then the grand tour of Europe. You planned the whole trip, trying to hit as many interesting places as possible with our Eurail pass. Quite unlike pre-packaged tours, our trip offered unknowns and daily adventures. In Florence, we wanted to find a quaint restaurant in the back streets. After trooping up and down on the hilly cobblestones with no success, we gave up. Clutching *Europe on Five Dollars a Day*, we found a kind-faced old gentleman and asked for directions. He looked at the first one of our three listed restaurants and said, "Roma." We had even got the city wrong! The second one earned another "Roma," and looking at the third one, he exploded angrily, "Roma!" With red faces, we ran away as fast as we could, muttering, "Sorry, sorry." From then on, if someone made an obvious mistake in the family, the others yelled in unison, "Roma!" The kids loved it.

We had our share of fighting as well. Hup used to tease us, "Weekdays, too busy; weekends, time to fight." There was never any major issue, only small stuff that I can't recall now. Those were the squabbles of young people who were blessed with so much, but didn't realize it—young people who hadn't yet tasted the overwhelming hardships life can deal out.

You took fatherhood seriously and were much more of a disciplinarian than I was. When Duncan, Monona, and I get together, we often reminisce and laugh about your "tiger dad" moments. Remember the time you got mad on a wintry Sunday morning when the kids were about six and four? They were making a racket downstairs, and Hup was having trouble controlling them. You jumped out of bed, grabbed the kids' snowsuits, stuffed them inside, then pushed them out into the cold garage. I thought you would break their little arms. Hup was beside herself yelling, "Teddy, Teddy, enough, enough!" The kids were scared all right, standing in the garage like two life-size dolls. That got us a quiet and obedient Sunday and endless memories for years to come.

Duncan adored you; he never bore any grudge when you punished him roughly. When the four of us played games, he always wanted you to win. For years after you were gone, he called me faithfully on your birthday. You're still alive among the three of us. Your children never ceased asking questions about you, "Did Daddy do this?"; "What do you think Dad would do?"; "Whom do you think Dad would vote for?"

As a father, you could be so loving and giving. You took the kids to swimming lessons, Indian Guides, the school fair, and shopping for Christmas trees and gifts. While I tried to dodge these "duties," you did them all happily, as if they were the most important activities on earth. You had such dreams for Duncan and Monona. You said to me once, "In all my life, the one perfect thing I am blessed with is our two children. I couldn't improve them even if I wanted to."

Your career at DuPont was going well. You were slated for promotion. We started to think about building a new house. One Sunday, after driving alone for hours looking at properties, you came home to drag me out of bed. Grumbling, I reluctantly went to see the lot that you had found. It was beautiful! We bought the land not much later and had blueprints drawn up for the house at the top of the hill. I have kept them to this day to remind me of when we were young, happy and full of hope.

In 1969, you got a sabbatical leave to teach at Taiwan University for a semester. You did that for me so I could be with my parents and they could enjoy the children. Indeed, we did have six months of joyous time together. You and I had fun by ourselves too, ending with an impressive tour of the island, the last of our many travels together. We lived in university housing for visiting professors until that horrible evening. You were soaking in a full tub of water, a habit you had developed in your army days. You didn't realize that in Taiwan bathroom heaters could leak carbon monoxide. The toxic gas made you drowsy, and you drowned while your loved ones were just in the next room.

The night you died and the next morning, when I had to tell the children, were the darkest hours of my life. My head swam, and I couldn't grasp the new reality. My parents did everything to help; the children and I moved in with them while Hup went to be with her sister. But nothing helped the confusion and the pain.

The children resumed their schooling; I would pace the floor all afternoon, waiting for them to come home. I was so relieved when I spotted them—a shipwrecked person suddenly spying fellow survivors wading toward her lonely island—and then I would be in tears as my heart broke for those fatherless two, so young and frail.

My emotions were on a rollercoaster for a long time. One moment I would grieve for your young life—that you would miss so much and we would miss so much of you. The next moment, I was consumed with regret that I didn't do enough for you, recalling every instance when I could have been more loving. I couldn't stop asking the useless questions, "Why, why, and why? How could fate be so cruel?" I was mad at Taiwan for their defective gas heaters, lousy emergency service, and much more. There were times when I was angry at you, too. I would say, "You come back and trade places with me. I'm willing to die and let you deal with this much pain and fear." In the end, the only thing left was the grief that blanketed me every morning before I was fully awake and refused to leave until sleep took over.

My parents wanted us to stay on in Taiwan, but I knew the kids would have a better future in the U.S. Besides, I just couldn't stay in Taiwan, where my love was taken away in a horrible accident and I felt like a total stranger. Eventually, my mother accompanied us back to Wilmington, to a home without you. The only thing that sustained me was my determination to take care of our children.

Sadness and grief hung over our house, but the children were amazing. Dealing with their own loss, they were sensitive to Hup's and mine. They were quiet and obedient. Monona told me years later about their frustration in not being able to ease our pain. Yet, being children, they also had unrepressed spirits—they told school jokes, described funny classmates and even teachers. Hup and I eagerly waited for their stories at the dinner table; their laughter lifted our spirits.

My favorite was the dining hall riot because I had never heard of such a thing in China. The kids vividly described how soup trickled down someone's shirt and pats of butter stuck to the ceiling. The cafeteria staff were at a loss as to what to do.

Finally, someone got the bright idea of getting "Mr. Ski." The impressive Mr. Wierzbowski, the shop teacher, stood over six feet tall and was strong and stern. He grabbed a large baseball bat, walked into the dining hall, and smashed it with a terrifying sound on the first table. He yelled with a booming voice, "Be quiet!" Like magic, that was the end of the food fight! Under his gaze, the students filed out, many with food still dripping from their hair and clothes.

With the help of the children, we reassembled as a family of four. We developed a good routine. At bedtime, I would sit with Duncan or Monona on alternate nights. They talked—about their day, their friends, schoolwork, and what they thought; I mostly listened. Duncan came up with such jewels as, "I looked up how many children don't have fathers. If they can make it, so can I." Monona talked about being pushed around by the older boys, being called "China face," but she didn't want me to go and talk to her teacher. I think that experience eventually made her the strong woman she is today, working against all things unjust. I, more than the children, benefited from these intimate talks, reassured that our strong bond and love would see us through all hardships. This routine eventually stopped on its own, an indication that a little normalcy had come back to our lives.

Gradually the gloom in our home lifted. We celebrated Duncan's birthday every year with exactly the same menu—spaghetti and meatballs—and exactly the same football game afterward. The boys and Monona would run all over the Snyders' large yard next door. Monona had sleepover parties with her girlfriends; they had to continually fend off Duncan's tricks to scare them in the dark.

A year after you were gone, a kind friend took me to Arden, which had a thriving international folk dance scene. Hup gave me her blessing. She knew, more than I did, that I needed something to do besides working and caring for the kids. I can never thank her enough for her support. I was even in a women's performing group for a few years. Folk dancing became my never waning passion, and it sustained me through the ups and downs of my work at DuPont and eventually, the deaths of my beloved elders.

We took family vacations, a couple of times on the same cruise ship line that you and I first traveled on together. Cruises were relaxing for us; Hup didn't have to rush in the morning nor go on the land tours she had no interest in. Yet we could be together, dressing up for dinners and doing activities on the ship. Once, we heard about a "horse race" on board. You could buy tickets with any combination of two numbers—one through six. Whoever correctly picked the first two wooden horses to finish in order would win all the money that was bet. Duncan figured out that, if he bought all thirty-six combinations, he would still come out ahead if more than a certain number of tickets were sold. He explained his logic to me, and I liked his mathematical thinking. I encouraged him to find out from the hostesses how many tickets were usually sold and how often there were double or triple winners. The hostesses all thought he was a cute fourteen-year-old and helped him with the answers. I made a pact with him that I would loan him the money to buy the tickets, but he had to give the winnings back to me because it was a math experiment and not gambling. He did win, with Hup, Monona and me cheering—a highlight of our trip. And I did take his winnings!

Our kids were always outstanding students. I used to enjoy going to PTA meetings at our elementary school; their teachers had only good things to say about them. Dr. Goode, the principal, said to me, "Mrs. Yin, please send us more good students like Duncan and Monona. We need good students." Years later, a stranger I chanced to talk to on the street still remembered that I was the mother of Duncan and Monona Yin. In high school, Duncan was the school wit and state chess champion; Monona, the scholar-athlete. She ran track and represented Brandywine High School in the state championships. You should have seen her run! Field hockey was her second love, and she made the all-conference team. They were good kids, hardly giving Hup and me any trouble, even through their teen years. They got themselves into Princeton and Yale, taking the tests and driving around to visit the campuses without much help from me at all. The funny thing was that I had expected no less from them.

Monona took her junior year abroad in Taiwan, living with my mother. My heart sang as I thought how the two people I loved most were getting to know each better. Monona learned Chinese and immersed herself in the culture; Grandma savored every moment of their togetherness.

Duncan looks just like you, but taller and bigger. When the kids went to China in 1999 and visited the Yin relatives, the older ones were all astonished at the resemblance. Monona looks more like me but has your thin fingers and long legs. Sometimes when they were teenagers, standing together like tall young trees, my heart would burst with pride.

The children loved Hup. At her 90th birthday celebration, they both gave speeches about how important Hup was to them. When she became very ill later that year, we three nursed her at home at the very end. Later, we honored her with a beautiful memorial.

Ted, I am sorry you missed the fun and pride the children gave to Hup and me. They were good children: intelligent, caring and devoted to our family. You didn't get to be the proud father at their graduations, nor the one to walk Monona down the aisle. Duncan and I did that. What a wedding! She put on a show with her drumming group, and danced a bride's dance from Eastern Europe with her many girlfriends; I had fun teaching them. Monona was supposed to sit in the middle of the circle as the bride—bittersweet at having to leave her village. Of course, she felt only happiness and insisted on doing the dance with the rest of us, so we let her.

Seven years later, Duncan's wedding was more formal but just as festive. I thought you would have made a handsome father-of-the-groom, silver-haired but still dashing. And yes, you would have made a doting grandpa when the grandchildren came.

Dear Ted, Duncan, Monona and I are still a family, along with their own families, sharing you and missing you, but happy nonetheless. As I grow older, your image in my mind may have faded as have some of the memories of our life together, but I am comforted by knowing that the bond between us will always remain strong because our good children—yours and mine—are our connection. That will never change.

Acknowledgements

I wrote all but the last two pieces in this collection for a writing course at the Academy of Lifelong Learning, University of Delaware, beginning in 1995. I am grateful to my instructors, Ann Gallagher and Kate Bowen, for offering helpful critiques and fortifying my self-confidence. On the long road to finishing this project, my writing friends: Nina Schafer, Frances Buttemheim, Karen Heyman, Regina and Ralph Allen, and Alice Shechter, all gave valuable feedback. I was also lucky to have Pamela Goffinet and her son Talbot Zabel work closely with me on the initial design of the book. I thank you all—not just for help with this project— but for your friendship and unwavering support.

My cousins-in-law, Donna and Lucy Yin, have been loving sisters to me for over fifty years and confirmed key points of family history. I am also grateful to my longtime friends Helen Tang Yates, Margaret and James Wang, Georgi and Mark Marquisee, Tricia Watson, and members of my women's group in Wilmington. You have all enriched my life so much.

My sincere appreciation goes to Sara Dougherty-Jones and her students in the New Neighbors English Language Learner program of The Campagna Center in Alexandria, VA. I have known Sara since she and Monona became friends in elementary school. Prior to publication, Sara assigned six chapters of this book to her advanced students, and I video chatted with them twice. It was deeply moving to learn that my experiences resonate with other immigrant women from all over the world.

Dancing has sustained me body and spirit since the 1970s. I would like to thank all of my dancing friends for countless hours of joy and friendship. Among them, David Hamilton has also supported my writing from the beginning. He has always been ready to correct my grammar over the years, making my English sound less like a translation from Chinese. More than this, Dave has given me long years of companionship; I am indebted to him for his devoted care in the last two years especially.

My dear children Duncan and Monona, son-in-law Steve Fahrer, and granddaughter Maya have cared for me with love and thoughtfulness. Daughter-in-law Amanda Boyd Yin and granddaughter Allison also gave me support and encouragement.

After I moved into Monona's home in Brooklyn in January 2016, she devoted herself to my well-being and desire to finish this project; she cooked for me, walked with me, helped manage my many medical needs, and made sure I felt loved. She cheered me on in my writing. Daily we sat together; we probed each remembered story, checked references, made hard choices about photos, and discussed every aspect of the book: its name, content, cover design and so forth. She devoted long hours, with her perfectionist's nature and ear for the language, to improving the readability of every chapter repeatedly until the final draft. She deserves more than a co-authorship! Working together on this collection has deepened our already close relationship; I am grateful for this rare blessing. We are the keepers of our family history.

I love you, my dear family, and this book is for you.

Family Timeline

1899 Father Gunsun Hoh born in Caodian, Jiangsu Province.

1901 Mother Tze Kao born in Nantong, Jiangsu.

1905 Father-in-law Ven-Long Yin born in Shanghai.

1906 Mother-in-law Yue-Fang Sun born in Shanghai.

1911 Qing Dynasty falls, Republic of China declared.

1923 Gunsun graduates from Springfield College, MA; Tze completes two years of study at University of Wisconsin; both return to China to begin teaching physical education at series of universities in Shanghai, Beijing, and Wuhan.

1924 Gunsun organizes National Athletic Meet in Wuhan.

1926 Ven-Long graduates from St. John's University, Shanghai.

1927 Chinese Civil War begins between Nationalists and Communists.

1929 Gunsun and Tze marry in Beijing, move to Manchuria.
Ven-Long and Yue-Fang marry in Shanghai, move to Hankou.

1930 Husband Theodore (Ted) Yin born in Hankou; Ven Long dies in airplane crash six days later; Yue-Fang and Ted return to Yin family home in Shanghai.

1931 Japan invades Manchuria; Gunsun and Tze flee Shenyang for Beijing.

1932 Author Fay Hoh born in Beijing.

1933 Hoh-Kao family moves to Qingdao, then Nanjing; Gunsun becomes Supervisor of Physical Education, National Ministry of Education.

1936 Summer Olympics in Berlin; Dorothy and Gunsun attend as part of Chinese delegation.

1937	Sino-Japanese War officially declared; Hoh-Kao family flees Nanjing for Chongqing just before Rape of Nanjing.
	Ted enrolls as one of first eight students at World School, Shanghai.
1940	Hoh-Kao family survives three years of bombing in Chongqing, moves to Qingmuguan (Greenwood Fort) in Sichuan Province.
1945	Japan surrenders and returns Taiwan to China; Chinese Civil War resumes.
1946	Hoh-Kao family moves back to Nanjing.
1948	Summer Olympics in London; Gunsun represents Nationalist China and becomes a co-founder of the Asian Games.
1949	Hoh-Kao family moves to Hsinchu, Taiwan; Tze becomes Principal of Hsinchu Elementary School.
1950	Ted moves to Hong Kong with uncle's family; Yue-Fang stays behind.
1952	Fay moves to US to study at Western College for Women in Ohio, later transfers to University of Wisconsin in Madison.
1953	Yue-Fang finally secures visa, moves to Hong Kong.
	Ted graduates from University of Hong Kong.
1954	Fay graduates from University of Wisconsin with BA in Chemistry.
1956	Tze becomes Founding Director, Elementary Teachers' In-Service Training Center, Banqiao, Taiwan.
1957	Ted earns MS degree from University of Alberta in Calgary, begins PhD program at University of Wisconsin.
1959	Fay and Ted marry, Berkeley Heights, New Jersey.
1960	Son Duncan born; Ted and Fay both receive doctorates; family moves to Wilmington, Delaware; Ted becomes physical chemist at DuPont Co.
1962	Daughter Monona born in Wilmington; Yue-Fang (Hup) joins family in US six months later.

1966	Fay becomes virologist at DuPont.
1967	Tze gives talk at World Education Conference in Asilomar, California.
1969	Ted takes sabbatical, teaches at National Taiwan University.
1970	Ted dies in accident in Taibei; Fay, Duncan, Monona and Hup return to Wilmington.
1971	Gunsun retires from National Ministry of Education.
1973	Gunsun receives Distinguished Alumnus Award from Springfield College.
1974	Tze retires from Elementary Teachers' In-Service Center.
1975	Gunsun struck by motorcycle, dies in Taibei.
1976	Tze becomes Vice President of Chinese Culture University, Taibei.
1982	Monona lives with grandmother Tze and great-aunt Yen in Taiwan.
1983	Tze receives honorary doctorate from Dankook University, South Korea.
1991	Fay retires from DuPont.
1992	Tze retires from Chinese Culture University.
1997	Yue-Fang and Tze die six weeks apart.
1998	Monona and Steve Fahrer marry in Brooklyn, NY.
2001	Granddaughter Maya Yin Fahrer born in Manhattan, NY.
2007	Duncan and Amanda Morley Boyd marry in Brooklyn, NY.
2009	Granddaughter Allison Fay Morley Yin born in Stamford, CT.

Family Names

Family	Relationship to Author	Chinese	Pinyin	Wade-Giles/Other
HOH	*grandfather*	郝鶴九	Hao Hejiu	He-Chiu Hoh
	grandmother	邱秋山	Qiu Qui-Shan	Ch'iu-Shan Ch'iu
	father	郝更生	Hao Gengsheng	Gunsun Hoh
	self	郝飛	Hao Fei	Fay Hoh
	brother	郝翔	Hao Xiang	Hsiang Hoh
KAO	*grandfather*	高楚秋	Gao Chuqiu	Ch'u-Ch'iu Kao
	grandmother	齊蓮	Qi Lian	Lien Ch'i
	mother	高梓	Gao Zi	Tze Kao
	aunt	高梣	Gao Yen	Yen Kao
	cousin	高德	Gao De	Te Kao

Family	Relationship to Author	Chinese	Pinyin	Wade-Giles/Other
YIN	*husband's grandfather*	殷仰之	Yin Yangzhi	Yang-Zhi Yin
	husband's grandmother	貝氏	Bei ( )	( ) Pei
	father-in-law	殷文龍	Yin Wenlong	Ven-Long Yin
	husband	殷本榮	Yin Benrong	Theodore Peng-Jung Yin
	son	殷安石	Yin Anshi	Duncan An-Shea Yin
	daughter	殷安中	Yin Anzhong	Monona An-Chung Yin
SUN	*husband's grandfather*	孫少甫	Sun Shaofu	Shao-Fu Sun
	husband's grandmother	沙懷英	Sha Huaiying	Huai-Ying Sha
	mother-in-law	孫月芳	Sun Yuefang	Yue-Fang Sun

215

Chinese Sayings

From left: son Duncan, granddaughter Allison, daughter-in-law Amanda, the author, daughter Monona, granddaughter Maya and son-in-law Steve.

About the Author

FAY HOH YIN was born in Beijing in 1932 to a family of educators. She grew up while China was wracked by almost two decades of war—first with Japan and then civil war between the Chinese Nationalists and Communists. She and her family fled thousands of miles to escape the chaos, finally settling in Taiwan in 1949. Two years later, she came to the U.S. as a foreign student and earned a Ph.D. in biochemistry from the University of Wisconsin. Fay married Ted Yin in 1959 and they had a son and daughter. After being widowed in 1970, she took up international folk dancing, which remained her passion for more than forty years. Fay retired in 1991 after working for twenty-six years as a virologist for the DuPont Company in Wilmington, Delaware.